INSIDE THE MIND OF A SERIAL RAPIST

Dennis J. Stevens, Ph.D

INSIDE THE MIND OF A SERIAL RAPIST

Dennis J. Stevens, Ph.D

Authors Choice Press

San Jose New York Lincoln Shanghai

Inside the Mind of a Serial Rapist

Authors Choice Press
an imprint of iUniverse.com, Inc.

For information address:
iUniverse.com, Inc.
5220 S 16th, Ste. 200
Lincoln, NE 68512
www.iuniverse.com

Originally published by Austin & Winfield

ISBN: 0-595-14663-5

Printed in the United States of America

Dedication

**Dedicated to all the little women in my life
my daughter, Alyssa Stevens
and my granddaughter, Danielle Stevens**

TABLE OF CONTENTS

Chapter 3
Rival Causes of Serial Rape

Chapter 4
Motives of Serial Rape: Lust, Righteous, and Peer Rape

Chapter 5
Motives of Serial Rape: Control/Anger, Supremacy,
Fantasy Rape, and Unclear

Chapter 6
Victim Selection Techniques

Chapter 7
Violence and Serial Rape

Chapter 8
Excessive Force

Chapter 9

Chapter 10

Appendix 1

Appendix 2

Appendix 3

Appendix 4

x

Appendix 5

LIST OF TABLES

COMMENDATORY FOREWORDS

Frank Schmalleger, Ph.D.

In *Inside the Mind of a Serial Rapist*, Dennis J. Stevens provides what may be the most realistic and comprehensive approach to the study of rape and serial rapists available to readers today. Rape, says Stevens, is far too often understood only in highly politicized terms. The jargon and perspectives that have been developed over the past 30 years to understand the motivations of rapists, Stevens tells us, have too frequently been built upon idealized political and social posturing by special interest groups. Such arm-chair theorizing, while it may lend itself to politically correct explanations of rape, is commonly removed from the realm of offender motivation, and the reality of rape itself.

Stevens analyzes traditional beliefs about rape by asking questions such as: "Is rape a tool of male power intended to keep women in subservient roles, or is it the carnal expression of lust subjectively experienced and acted upon by inadequately socialized individuals?

Most instructive is Stevens' use of participant self-reports; that is, information from rapists themselves – collected through interviews with more than 60 serial offenders. Interestingly, Stevens' methodology was to employ convicted felons as interviewers in order to avoid being "conned" by his subjects. Stevens sets the theme for the entire book in the preface when he writes, "My aim is to tell you what I have learned about this crime from the mouths of men who have committed it."

Stevens' debunking of rape "myths," especially those which lead to fear and passivity among victims, is worthwhile reading all by itself because it questions many contemporary assumptions about rape. According to Stevens, debunking such myths empowers women, making them more capable of successfully avoiding and resisting rape.

Especially worthwhile, however, is the qualitative interview information that Stevens has gathered. As a result of intimate interviews with actual rapists, *Inside the Mind of a Serial Rapist* sheds new light on how rapists think and feel about their crimes, on what motivates them to commit such offenses, and on how they select their targets. Some of Stevens' findings are bound to surprise you!

Inside the Mind of a Serial Rapist offers a fresh, close-to-the-source, form of understanding about rape. Chapters such as "Inside the Head of a Rapist" are replete with insights into the thought processes and world views of rapists. Moreover, the subjective understandings of offender motivation developed by Stevens lead to new typologies of rapists, rapist motivations, and rape victims. Stevens' typologies offer insightful guidance for future research, and can surely help policy makers in planning programs to prevent rape as well as in the handling of convicted rapists.

Inside the Mind of a Serial Rapist provides a fresh perspective on the crime of forcible rape – and the motivation behind. This book is a "must read" for anyone interested in better understanding this often misinterpreted crime.

Frank Schmalleger, Ph.D.
Director
The Justice Research Association

FOREWORD

M.L. Dantzker, Ph.D.

Rape—regardless of definition, or how, where, and why it is committed, or who commits it—is a heinous and demoralizing crime. Despite the nature of the crime, a mixture of violence, power, intimidation, and sexual innuendo, it has long been viewed as a crime of power and domination over females by males. This has resulted in a plethora of literature among academic sources and the popular press that have tended to perpetuate the idea that rape is committed purely to placate man's savage need to control women. However, a more realistic look at rape in today's world finds that it is not limited to men raping women, but includes men raping men, men raping children, women raping children, and yes, even women raping women. With all these possibilities, the idea that rape is purely a power and domination activity, begins to lose some of its potency. Still, rape is a predominant male versus female crime which is why the bulk of theories and concepts for why rapes occur remains focused on the idea that it is man's desire to belittle and demoralize women. Few seem to want to challenge this position, until now.

In this book, *Inside the Mind of the Serial Rapist,* Dr. Dennis J. Stevens steps outside the circle of conformity and acquiescence and offers a view of rape many would rather ignore, that it may be more a sexual crime than a violent or power crime. In offering this view, Dr. Stevens does not provide conjecture, hypothesis, or theory, but supplies facts from those who might best be able to explain why rapes happen, the rapist.

Through interviews of 61 convicted rapists Dr. Stevens explores why such crimes were committed and as a result challenges the long-standing ideas or myths surrounding the crime of rape. This is done in an academic and open manner that is both intriguing and thought-provoking. While Dr. Stevens does not claim that current theories and beliefs about why rape occurs are wrong, he does strongly suggest that thought should be given to the possibilities that there are more sexually-related causes to rape than some might care to acknowledge. His research even shows some support for the longstanding causes, but adds the dimension some might whisper among themselves but generally fear to say openly, that sexual attractiveness and vulnerability are extremely real components to rape, especially among the serial rapists.

Overall, Dr. Stevens has presented a new look at an age old crime using information not gleamed from reports or believes but from the people who best know why they commit rape. By providing this work, he has offered another means for examining criminality and for possibly gaining better insight into a crime few of us find anything but pathetic and horrible. While I do not expect everyone to agree with Dr. Stevens' insights and findings, I do trust that everyone who reads this with an open mind will find themselves having to think, perhaps there is more to the act of rape than just power, violence, and dominance.

M.L. Dantzker, Ph.D.
University of Texas- Pan American

ACKNOWLEDGEMENTS

Thomas B. Priest at Johnson C. Smith University provided inspiration to complete this work. Michael Shone at the University of South Carolina and Don C. Gibbons at Portland State College spent considerable time editing parts of the materials which eventually became chapters in this work. Sammy Catch from Mount Olive College helped with the fuzzy parts of the conclusion.

The author wishes to thank the men and the women of the South Carolina, North Carolina, Illinois and New York Departments of Corrections for their help. A special thanks to inmates William Grace and Thomas D. Crooks, Jr. who kept my head on my shoulder more than once.

My mother Joann Stevens, my sister Suzanne Koller, my sons David and Mark and my wife, Cindy, delivered frequent encouragement. Lastly, every time I held my beautiful daughter Alyssa, I was driven to complete these pages.

Grateful acknowledgement is given to the following publications in which articles in this volume originally appeared.

Stevens, D.J. (1994). "Predatory Rape and Victim Targeting Techniques," *The Social Science Journal*, 31 (4), 421-433. 1994.

Stevens, D.J. (1995). "Motives of Serial Rapists," *Free Inquiry in Creative Sociology*, 23(2), 117-126. 1995.

Stevens, D.J. (1997). "Violence and Serial Rape," *Journal of Police and Criminal Psychology*, 12(1), 39-47. 1997.

Stevens, D.J. (1998). "Explanations of Excessive Force Used During Serial Rape Attacks," *Criminologist*. In Press. 1998.

INTRODUCTION

This book is about serial rapists. It will tell you what I have learned about
this crime from the mouths of the men who have committed it. It all started one
day while I was dashing up the stairs to my criminal justice class at the University
of South Carolina, Aiken. I froze in stride when a huge sign shouted these words
at me: ALL MEN ARE POTENTIAL RAPISTS. BEWARE! After reading
many articles on the subject, I decided that the power brokers turned the study of
rape into a political obsession instead of a criminal investigation. Rape, they said,
is a devise used by aggressive men to enslave women. I guessed that some women
were no longer willing to accept the lead of aggressive men. Maybe they're right,
but not all men want to control women. Angry women. and some should be, think
so. Now, as evidenced by the sign at the top of the stairs, some angry women
were stirring concerns inside me demanding inquiry.

Go To The Source

I recalled earlier advice given by my professors at Loyola University of
Chicago who explained that when a researcher wants to inquire about something,
go to the source. They argued that secondary sources could alter truth. I took that
to mean that if I want to know if students are happy, don't ask parents or teachers,
ask students. If I want to know about crime. ask the experts-by-experience—
criminals. I did. In fact, I also trained inmate-students to ask other criminally
violent offenders about predatory rape. One conclusion I came away with was that
this book had to be written.

Believing Criminals

Although criminals lie, there is something to be heard from them. The real question is why would they lie about criminal activities especially if an inmate is telling his stories to another convicted felon? Would stories about a crime make other inmates admire or despise him? If you're an resident of a maximum custody penitentiary with a lot of time on your hands and living daily with 1,500 of the worst lot of men, what would you tell them?

    A. Build your criminal ventures

    B. Keep a low profile

    C. Brag about beating grandmothers into sexual submission

    D. Reveal stories that could hurt parole opportunities

    E. Tell stories about sexual encounters with children

Selection 'B' is probably a prudent response. Would you exaggerate the circumstances of a crime you were never tried for, knowing prosecution could be near? The truth is that it is hard to get a rapist to talk about his criminal activities particularly if he has never been charged with the crime. Inmates have two jobs in prison. One job is to keep a clean record in order to be released. Making up stories to look good to another inmate would not get you back on the street faster.

In general, rapists are looked upon as "weak," said William Grace, one of two lifers who helped guide my work, and who protected my interests on several occasions. "First," he said, "if they were convicted for rape that means they didn't have control of their women. Second, they had to resort to short cuts to get sex. Only wimps need to attack for sex," he added. Thomas Crooks Jr., another inmate I am indebted too, advised that "in prisons like this, being macho means survival, and part of machismo is having ladies around when you were on the street that loved your ass." That's the other job inmates have in maximum custody confinement—survival. Convicted rapists are usually segregated from the other prisoners as they come under attack a lot of the time, especially men who raped children.

When I worked at Stateville, a notorious maximum custody penitentiary near Chicago, the prisoners bet that the life of John Wayne Gacy would end in less than 52 seconds if he were in general prison population. His living quarters were segregated from all other inmates, and he was guarded 24 hours a day, 7 days a week by a special task force of correctional officers.[1] On the other hand, at the same penitentiary, Richard Speck, who had viscously attacked, raped, and killed several nurses. was a prison painter and worked on the walls outside my prison classroom at Stateville. Speck was safe in general prison population. Inmates have their own sense of justice.

While there are always exceptions to every rule, it appears that the accounts of rape by incarcerated inmates might be underestimates of their activities. Other researchers also find that rapists tend to say less about sexual offenses than other inmate offenders do.[2]

However, being suspicious of criminals is always a good idea because they are, indeed, criminals! Yet, as you examine their narratives in this work, remember that there are limitations of those narratives as they relate only to apprehended criminals and serial rapists, not to other types of criminals or to other types of rapists. Clearly, fresh ways of getting at the truth of rape-behavior is obscured by both rape-politics and myths produced by fear entrepreneurs who sensationalize serial rape. But. by ignoring narratives offered by serial rapists, is it possible that knowledge could be lost? Or do we move forward and borrow a thought from Palmer who says:

> Rape is prevented by accurate knowledge about its causes, and the objective examination of evidence and the skeptical evaluation of conclusions based on that evidence could only obtain accurate knowledge.[3]

Yet, it is odd when some researchers talk about past experiences and future expectations of serial rapists, they seem to combine all forms of rape activity or examine it in clinical laboratories. Sometimes researchers make general statements suggesting that the motivation for predatory rape and date rape is similar. A predator hunting victims down like dogs certainly has a different goal than a high school senior trying to impress his friends. If we ask victims or cops, or examine criminal files, each might have something important to share about how a predator picks prey. But. I also want to hear from individuals who have done the hunting before I feel that I've learned something about the hunt.

Sharing Some Thoughts

Let me share some of my personal thoughts with you about the attacks of the predatory rapists I interviewed in this study. During the study, I experienced a variety of feelings. First, I felt pain and helpless to comfort their victims. Second, I prayed for the power to help their victims, but realized there was nothing I could do to change the experiences faced by those individuals. Third, I felt frustrated that some individuals could irrevocably alter the experiences of innocent people and angry that some of those self-centered predators felt pity and remorse for their victims. Fourth, I felt the horror of submission of their victims and wished there were something I could do to prevent future victimization. Fifth, after many sessions with those criminally violent offenders, I thought I was tough but I often caught myself crying in my car on my way home from prison.

Uniqueness of this study

Some psychologists, sociologists, and/or retired FBI agents examined the nuances of serial rape much like sliding a Buick through the eye of a needle. They developed reasonable theories about serial rapists in their offices. They collected and analyzed information at police stations and libraries and linked those findings to support existing popular viewpoints about serial rapists. What makes my work unique is that I reversed the process and let the theory arise from the information I gained in the penitentiary. In this study I: 1) exclusively examined serial rape; (2) let serial rapists speak for themselves rather than asking victims or reviewing records; (3) and obtained data through convicted felons trained as interviewers. Ideas about rape motivation, target selection, and violence emerged from the offenders. Law enforcement officers, correctional case workers, and criminologists helped evaluate the stories of the offenders, and solutions to curb serial rape came from offenders rather then psychologists, sociologists. or FBI agents.

Chapter Order

This book is arranged in such a way as to guide you through the number of complex issues surrounding serial rape. Chapter 1 is an introduction to serial rape. it discusses the typical victim, the number of predatory rape attacks, and offers some insights as to why victims do not report predatory rape. Chapter 2 presents some general myths about predatory rape and information about how to control it: for instance, there is a discussion on articles in popular women magazines which encourages victim submission while promoting and reinforcing a learned helplessness among women. Chapter 3 considers a number of rival theories that try to explain predatory rape but miss reality. Chapter 4 offers explanations of serial rape motivation through the categories of lustful rape, righteous rape, and peer rape. Chapter 5 gives explanations of serial rape motivation through the categories of control/anger rape, supremacy rape, and fantasy rape. Chapter 6 discusses victim selection techniques used by predators and how to avoid rape. Chapter 7 clarifies a serial rapist's use of physical force and Chapter 8 explains why some offenders use excessive force, commit necrophilla. and cannibalism.

6

This chapter includes a discussion on why predators embrace evil during some of their ruthless attacks, suggesting that sexual offenders may well have a sexual addiction. Chapter 9 offers a narrative about the daily life of a serial rapist. Chapter 10 offers a conclusion and recommendations based on the findings of this work including the use of drugs to chemically castrate sexual offenders as one method of dealing with sexual addiction.

Appendix 1 gives a description of the prison where this study was conducted. Appendix 2 discusses the research design or method used and information about how the sample was obtained, about the student-interview design, and about criminal validity. Appendix 3 shows the types of questions used during the interview process. Appendix 4 describes the characteristics of the offenders in the sample and includes a table for your convenience. And Appendix 5 discusses the race of the victims. There are five tables in this book to help guide you through this complex issue: Table 1 on inmates admitting to serial rape, Table 2 on the rape categories, Table 3 on target selection methods. Table 4 is a typology of violence, and Table 5 in Appendix 4 shows the demographics of the sample used in this study.

Objectives

I have related in this book to the major interpretations of serial rape offered by the popular writers in the field and have given a comprehensive view about serial rape from the perspective of the offenders. The evidence suggests that "fear entrepreneurs" promote and reinforce both a fear of rape and a learned helplessness among females that aid predators during their attacks. The evidence suggests that politically correct theory has little to do with criminal reality and less to do with crime control. It will become clear that serial rape is not a single isolated event in the life of a rapist, but that it is an ongoing series of conscious lifestyle decisions made by him. Some rapists embrace evil suggesting that

America is moving into an unhealthy and unholy society since public violence has become private violence and is heading toward collective violence. A velvet glove and dagger approach is necessary to control predators—effective prevention and persuasive punishment.

I have suggested how to avoid becoming a serial rape target, and provided insight into another one of our growing problems—a psychological dependence or addiction of forced sexual encounters with females. Sexual offenders cannot be rehabilitated; they must be controlled. At the conclusion of this book, the following recommendations are offered: classifying sexual offenders as addicts, chemical castration with drugs such as depo-provera, educating females about learned helplessness, identifying sexual offenders in the community, eliminating plea-bargaining, enhancing police power, mandatory life sentences in segregation, and frequent use of capital punishment.

About This Study

Thirteen inmate-students had been in a variety of classes and/or group sessions with me for over a year, prior to enrolling in a university course entitled Sociology of Crime. I trained all of them as student-interviewers for that class. They attended several lectures and participated in many classroom discussions on researcher bias and interviewing techniques over a fifteen-week period. Some of the ideas we discussed were subjects about interview techniques such as interviewees telling interviewers what interviewers wanted to hear whether research was conducted in a prison or in a shopping mall. We had practice sessions, too, which needless to say, were memorable. The inmate-interviewers were told not to tell other inmates what we were studying. Equally important, I never told the inmate-interviewers the information I sought. Besides. it would be many months after gathering all of the data and carefully studying it that I would

8

know what it all meant.[4] This study was comprised of 61 offenders who were incarcerated at a maximum custody penitentiary.[5]

Admitting Serial Rape

Among the 61 participants, 3% (2) of them admitted to at least fifty serial rapes each or a total of 100; 5% (3) offenders admitted to at least twenty-five serial rapes each or 75; 13% (8) admitted to ten serial rapes each or total of 80, 26% (16) of them admitted to two serial rapes each or 32; and 40% (24) admitted to one serial rape ech or 24 (see Table 1). The remaining 5% (3) offenders reported that their rape convictions "were a case of mistaken identity," while another 3% (2) said they had never committed rape, although all (5) of these participants had been convicted for sexual assault and each offered descriptions of serial rape during their interviews.[6] Therefore, based on the responses of 61 offenders, a conservative guess is that the sample attempted to at least 316 serial rapes or an average of 5 rapes per participant.

However, those figures may not be totally accurate. Men who commit predatory rape don't always see their crimes as an offense. When called upon to discuss their criminal activities, they give only those experiences they considered illegal. Other times, they simply lose track of their criminal activities. How accurate are their recollections of those past unimportant events? Collectively this group probably underestimated their attacks and committed closer to four times the number they discussed. That might put their real number of attacks at 1708 or 28 each.[7] Once these men are released, (and most of them have been at this writing) they will commit more violent crimes including serial rape largely due to their previous lifestyles prior to their incarceration and due in part to their experiences at prison.[8]

Table 1			Admitting Serial Rape				(N=61)	
Not Sure	Never Denied	Never Mistaken Identity	Once	Twice	10/More	25More	50/More
3%	5%	5%	40%	26%	13%	5%	3%

*Percents rounded

Statements of the Sample

The statements of the predators were not edited. Their explicit and vulgar language is neither encouraged nor appropriate for most of us; I wish to apologize for any discomfort you might experience when reading some of these pages. Most grammatical inconsistencies may be the error of the participants interviewed rather than the error of the writer. However, to edit their comments to fit what we consider acceptable might change the meaning of what the offenders have to say. All names used are fictitious.

[1] Gacy had buried the body parts of many young boys under his home in a suburb of Chicago. The State of Illinois finally put him to death (May 1994) almost 13 years after being captured. But, an inmate at Columbia Correctional in Wisconsin got to Jeffrey Dahmer despite protective custody and killed him on November 28, 1994. That entire episode took less than 60 seconds.

[2] For a closer review of this perspective see Scully (1990) and MacKinnon (1987).

[3] Crag Palmer (1988)

[4] For more detail about inmate student interviews and criminal validity see Appendix 2.

[5] See Appendix 3 for type of questions used during the interviews. See Appendix 4 for sample, date collection, interview design, and Table 5 showing the characteristics of the sample. See Appendix 5 for race of victims.

[6] Therefore, I'll count one serial rape for each of these offenders adding five to the estimated total.

[7] For a life time of crime, since the average age was 32 at the time of the interviews and most of the descriptions of the participants characterized what appeared to be criminal lifestyle experiences at 18, two rapes a year over a 14 year period (or an average of 28 serial rapes) might be closer to the truth.

10

[8]Both incarcerated female and male offenders tend to assimilate norms, values, and violence of prison and depending on individual prison time served, most nonviolent offenders will engage in a variety of violent crimes due to their prison experiences once released. For a closer look at female incarceration and anticipated crime see Stevens (1998c). To see male incarceration and anticipated crimes see Stevens (1994b, 1995b). To review predictors of violent offenders see Stevens (1997c). One hundred and eighty nine violent convicts and 124 nonviolent incarcerated participants at a maximum custody penitentiary in New York were surveyed. The results show that early childhood experiences centered on constant parent quarreling were the best predictors of violent offenders more often than nonviolent offenders.

CHAPTER ONE

Definition of Serial Rape

One official definition of rape is carnal knowledge through the use of force or the threat of force. When it happens more than once by the same offender, I call it serial rape. But sometimes serial rapists fail at their attempts and sometimes they do not perform sexual intercourse for many reasons including premature ejaculation, individual rationalizations, and/or a victim may put an end to the attack by fighting back or escaping. Serial rapists attack many females, some they know and some they don't. Sometimes serial rapists coerce others into submission through intimidation and manipulation. Sometimes they lie, misrepresent, or smooth talk victims into sexual encounters. In fact, a victim might think she is consenting of her own free-will to sexual contact with a serial rapist when in reality she had been led to believe a lie; other times, she might think she can control a serial rapist and discovers, much to her regret, she was easy pray. A lack of knowledgeable or informed consent is part of any efficient definition of rape. The terms serial and predatory are interchangeable descriptions of serial rape. Therefore, for the purposes of this work, predatory or serial rape refers to more than one coerced attempt or actual sexual contact of others without their informed consent.[1]

The Victim

The serial rapist can attack any aged female regardless of her physical condition or the company she is in. Predatory rapists attack females who are unconscious, recovering from surgery, young, old, attractive, or women whose physical attributes are unknown to them. They attack females in the process of

12

committing other felons such as break-ins and armed robberies. They attack white females more often black females. In 1995, approximately 240,820 white victims reported being rape victims as compared with 61,290 black victims, according to the Bureau of Justice Statistics.[2] An explanation is that white women report forcible rape more often than black women do. Black women in general have a lower opinion of law enforcement than do white women and may not be as confident with reporting it as others.

Predatory rapists attack females who are alone, females who are with friends, women with their husbands and children with their parents. They attack females when they work, walk, and even when they help others. They attack females who are in public places such as shopping malls. Private places such as restrooms and safe places such as recovery rooms at hospitals. But mostly, they attack females whom they perceive to be vulnerable or females whom they intimidate into a vulnerable situation.

How Many Victims Are There?

It's difficult to establish how many females have been raped since forcible rape statistics are confusing. There are many statistical equations available, and it's a matter of which one you want to believe. There are two reliable contributors to rape statistics: police reports and criminal victimization reports.

Police records are established from victim reports to local law enforcement agencies. Those agencies relate the information to the U.S. Department of Justice. They produce finalized reports, which are distributed through the Bureau of Justice Statistics (BJS). Criminal victimization rates are measures of the occurrence of victimization among a specified population group. Those results are also reported to the U.S. Department of Justice and published by BJS.[3]

BJS breaks down rape reports by stranger rape and non-stranger rape. For instance, they estimated that almost 175,000 rapes were reported to the police in

1995. Of those reports, approximately 52% (90,300) were stranger rapes. BJS showed that 30,480 were completed stranger rapes and 59,820 were attempted stranger rapes. They estimated that there were more rape attacks by strangers than non-strangers, but strangers failed at their attempts more often than did non-strangers.[4] Also, serial rapists attack females they knew such as their wives and their children.

Victimization reports show that almost 40% or another 70,000 victims never reported rape attacks to anyone including the police. Other estimators suggest that 60% of rape victims never report it. One reason for the difference in the two calculations could partly relate to difference in the understanding of what constitutes rape. For example, until 1993 South Carolina and many other states had not considered spouse rape an illegal act. States who had passed such a law rarely enforce it. Perhaps, some women felt since they couldn't report their spouse for rape why report a stranger?

Why Victims Don't Report Serial Rape

There are many reasons women don't report predatory rape. The Bureau of Justice Statistics guesses that 25% of the females who didn't report rape might say that their it was a personal matter while another 10% would say that they thought they lacked proof. Eleven percent of the non-reporters of rape might reveal that they were afraid of reprisals from their attacker. Also, 2% of those victims had not reported rape because they felt it was an unimportant event. Other reasons which the Bureau of Justice Statistics did not address might include shame, embarrassment, and the poor reputation of the police.

It might be safe to say that women fail to report being victimized out of fear of being victimized, again. That is, once a woman is raped and tells a spouse or boy friend, friends, and/or the criminal justice community, she is treated differently. She can be made to feel guilty. For instance, it is common practice for law enforcement, social workers, hospital personnel, and defense lawyers to question her lifestyle prior to the sexual assault. They think that her lifestyle before the attack had something to do with the crime.

Experience suggests that many victims fail to report all kinds of crimes including sexual assault in part due to feelings of self-blame. Victim self-blame or guilt may center on the way a victim dressed, smiled, or walked to her car after shopping at K-Mart. If she changed something about herself, she would have never been a target.

Since their fathers, brothers, husbands, ministers, and other women have treated females as inferior to males throughout most of their lives, she might consider her victimization as further proof of her inability to compete and to win against males.[5] Clearly, rape does not prove that a female is inferior or at fault. Nonetheless, many victims think that by not reporting crimes against themselves that they won't be considered losers. Lastly, some females. especially young girls, can't tell their parents about being victimized by strangers because their parents or guardians have themselves abused them.

Consequently, what all of the above means is that we may never know how many females. or for that matter how many males, have been sexually attacked by strangers. A good guess is that the number of rape attacks is far greater than anyone expects or wants to believe. It is surprising how often in the classroom females come forward and explain how they were victimized but hadn't reported it because they felt they had brought the rape upon themselves or because they were afraid others would treat them differently. Statistics can't change the events some individuals have experienced nor can some victims be left to themselves. Evidently many victims have little desire to come forward, even when the justice community has good intentions. In some cases, those victims shouldn't. For instance, research has shown that mandatory arrest of domestic violence offenders leads to more not less violence against victims.[6]

There are many problems surrounding the popular definition of rape and explaining the differences in police reports and victimization reports. How many rape victims there are is highly debatable. Clearly, the public has limited information to gage rape attacks. One reason it is difficult to tell the number of rapes is due in part to the apprehensiveness of victims and level of confidence they have in the criminal justice system. However, all estimates suggest that potential forcible rape attacks influence the way many women live. Other factors why women don't report rape could relate to their situation or their cultural expectations. For example, some victims feel that law enforcement is less likely to respond to rape reports in the poorer section of a community, thus those women might report it less often. Overall, it is difficult to determine the actual number of rape attacks due to the number of unreported cases; there are probably many more cases of rape unreported than expected. Yet some writers estimate that 1 in 5 females might be sexually attacked sometime in her life, and I estimate that one-half of those victims will be attacked by serial rapists.

[1] This definition is consistent with other scholarly definitions of stranger rape (Cohen et al., 1971; Groth, 1979). For more details, see Belknap (1996) who argues that there is a tendency to minimize or redefine situations that do not meet the criteria of the traditional definition of rape. Therefore, Belknap's definition of rape includes any sexual intimacy forced on one person by another.

[2] Bureau of Justice Statistics (BJS), (1997) shows that of the white victims, 122.700 rapes were completed and 118,120 failed (49%) as compared to 35,510 were completed and 25,380 failed (41%) among black victims. See Appendix 4 about the victims of this sample.

[3] BJS (1997). This reference is available online: http://www.albany.edu/sourcebook/ or victimization reports available online: http://www.albany.edu/sourcebook/1995/ind/VICTIMIZATION.Rape.Number.2.html or from the US Department of Justice by calling 1(800) 732-3277 and asking for NCJ1258900 (a $6.00 charge will apply).

[4] The Department of Justice does not use the term serial rapists or predatory rapists for stranger rapists. That is, they do not break down the number of times a predator has attacked females, because they don't know. They know the police report initiated by the victim or witnesses. Many stranger rapes are committed by

16

serial rapists—individuals sexually attacking many females. But stranger rape and serial rape are different incidents.

[5] Images of inferiority for females are communicated in many different forms and in an enormous range of contexts beginning at an early age. These images are found in children's movies like the *Lion King* depicting females in exclusively helper roles, television shows like NYPD Blue depicting female detectives as drunks and incompetent, experiences at school and at the work place where men play most of the major roles as administrators and leaders. See Stevens (1998a) for more detail. Also, women convicted of homicide report losing their assets such as home, savings accounts, and personal items including their children to in-laws or the courts leaving a serious gap in their experiences and their financial opportunities to defend themselves. Also, when a female is arrested for the murder of her spouse, his family takes all of her assets making it impossible to win visitation rights let alone her murder defense. Oddly, there appears to be a Kafkaesque inquiry into who feels the pains of imprisonment more severe females or males. See Stevens (1998b; 1998e) for more detail.

[6] Spouse abusers who were arrested intensified their victimization after an arrest. Some of the methods they used included: night attacks, possessions of the victims such as cars, telephones, and clothes were destroyed; victims were isolated from friends, parents, and bank/credit accounts; and victims met with sexual assault from foreign objects, friends, and in some cases the children of the abusers. Most of the officers who interacted with victims and offenders were reluctant to intervene; they were apprehensive to make an arrest despite evidence suggesting they should; surprisingly enough, their behavior during the intervention appeared hostile to victims. Also, arrest had not protected victims from abuse and when victims fled from their homes, many of them sought out other abusers. see Stevens (1998e).

CHAPTER TWO

MYTHS ABOUT RAPE

General Myths about Serial Rape

There are many legends or myths about serial rape and how to control it. This chapter examines seven common myths about predatory rape. My intention is to address a few of those myths and to answer anticipated questions about this crime. Experiences in the university classroom reflect something I refer to as the fear of rape. Many students admitted they have been taught from a very young age that if attacked, submit; otherwise, attackers would hurt them. Many of the rapists I interviewed for this study liked that idea and implied I should do nothing to destroy that myth. "Who spread that rumor, Richard Speck or the Boston Strangler?" William Grace asked.

Myth One:
Submitting When Sexually Attacked

Some writers believe that women should fear their attackers and comply with their demands.[1] They believe that predatory rape is largely rooted in male power trips, personality flaws, and/or uncontrollable urges for violence. Those advocates argue that a strong relationship exists between sexual assault, offender violence, and victim surrender. The mission of a rapist can include the complete physical degradation of a victim. Therefore, they imply that a female should submit when sexually attacked because her attacker is a person who enjoys violence more than sex.[2]

Consistent with this view are 141 articles about serial rape in the mainstream press from 1982 to 1995 which were reviewed for this study. Those publications include: *Ebony, Essence, Glamour, Good Housekeeping, Ladies Home Journal, Maclean's, Mademoiselle, McCalls, MS, Nations Business, Newsweek, NY Times Magazine, People Weekly, Psychology Today, Redbook, Reader's Digest, Scholastic Update, Time, Teen.*

Most of the titles on serial rape linked wanton violence and rape together. For example, "Three Fearful Hours" in *People Weekly*, "The War on Women" in *Scholastic Update*, "A Betrayal of Trust" in *Good Housekeeping*, "Violence Against Women" in *MS*, and "I Just Want to Live in *Reader's Di*gest. Other articles like "Why Do Men Rape" in *Glamour*, "Why Men Rape" in *Mademoiselle*, and "What's Behind the Dramatic Rise in Rapes" in *Ebony* report that power, anger, and torture are characterized in every rape and that violence is the main objective of the rapist, not sex. In the article, "Inside the Mind of a Rapist," a rapist implied that most of his victims did not fight back. The writer, Jeanie Kasindorf, relied upon the interpretation of a Brandeis psychologist who tied rape with sadism and anger. Part of her interpretation includes the perceptive that women should never fight back when attacked by a serial rapist because rapists are sadists who want to destroy women. In *Psychology Today* there are two articles. "Assertiveness Breeds Attempt" and "Eve's Punishment" which imply that women should play the role of a passive victim when attacked. Other articles depict heinous violence like "Fraternities of Fear: Gang Rape, Male Bonding, and the Silencing of Women" and "Femicide: Speaking the Unspeakable" in MS. These fear entrepreneurs, present similar messages as Caputi and Russell suggest in *MS* magazine:

> Rape is a direct expression of sexual politics, an assertion of masculinist norms, and a form of terrorism that preserves the gender status quo. ...Murder is simply the most extreme form of sexist terrorism.

Only 8 (6%) of 141 articles described resistance, and each of those articles emphasized delayed reaction. Of those articles discussing weapons, they said that only women who are gun experts should carry guns. The compelling evidence offered above promotes and reinforces both the fear of rape and a learned helplessness among many females. That is, females learn that they are helpless against the initial uncontrollable assault of rape and no matter what they do they lose. Dr. Judith Siegel in *Mademoiselle*, Dr. Hobson director of the sex offender programs at Connecticut Correctional Institute at Somers in *Ebony*, and Dr. Lizotte in *Glamour* all insist that fighting sexual attackers serves to antagonize the attacker and he will respond with more violence.

Newspapers, too, add to the fear of rape perspective by sensationalizing rape and violence.[3] Several major city newspapers purposely report rape in broad terms that intensify reader fears as most identify with the victims. Many readers see themselves as the victims when reading those broad termed articles. A newspaper reporter I know said that newspapers keep their articles about crime in broad terms to keep the identity of the victims confidential. Maybe so, but how often do victims remain unknown especially in celebrated cases like the victims of Mike Tyson, the Kennedy clan, and the Central Park attack in New York. Nonetheless, the press adds to the fear of rape with their sensationalization of rape and reinforces victim-learned helplessness.

The problem is that television and radio newscasters tend to use newspapers and magazines as exclusive sources for information they relay to the public. The public generally receives exaggerated accounts of the rapists. Therefore, these writers conclude that women who fight an attacker could be killing themselves.

In summary, newspaper and magazine articles victimize women. If these fear entrepreneurs are right, then most of serial rapists are violent men whose goal is nothing more than beating women senseless and any sexual behavior is incidental to their violence.

Myth Two:
Population Increases Causes More Serial Rape

Some population advocates believe that as the American population grows, so does the rate of serial rape. With more people—there is more crime. If they're right, population and predatory rape increases should be somewhat parallel in their escalation rates.

The American population in 1971 was 206,212,000. In 1991, it was 252,177,000. That's a gain of 45,965,000 or 22%. Therefore, if the population increases impact rape, then serial rape should show similar percentile increases over a twenty-year period.

In 1971, the U.S. Department of Justice reported 42,260 forcible rapes. In 1991, they reported 106,590 rapes. That is 64,330 more rapes twenty years later. This represents an increase of 152% rapes. Were more rapes reported in 1991 than in 1971? Surprisingly, more were reported in 1971 than in 1991 despite victimization reports showing that in 1971 approximately 49% of the rape victims reported as compared to 1991 when 59% reported. An explanation, in part, comes from surveys taken by the National Opinion Research Center in both 1973 (1971 isn't available) and 1991: fewer women in 1991 as opposed to 1973 had confidence in the police doing their jobs. Since more women were confident about police activities in 1971. it is reasonable that more of them reported rape then when they had less confidence in the police.

Nonetheless, 22% versus 152% says something about the idea that population and rape are related variables. A significant correlation is virtually nonexistent between the increases in the American population and the increases in forcible rape levels especially when in various cities where populations have decreased over a twenty year period like Chicago and Detroit, yet rape rates gained steadily gains according to government statistics.

Myth Three:
Legalizing Prostitution Would Result in Less Forcible Rape

If prostitution were legal, forcible rape would be reduced. In a sense, this myth implies that if prostitution were legal then there would be less forcible rape per capita (per 100,000 inhabitants) in areas where prostitution is legal as compared to areas where it is not legal. Reviewing forcible rape figures for Las Vegas, Nevada, a city serviced by legalized prostitution, there were 433 rapes in 1991. Las Vegas is a city like no other city in the United States as it attracts millions of tourists year around. However, cities like Miami, Honolulu, and New Orleans have many similarities to Las Vegas including a pleasant climate. But, Miami's rape rate was 253, Honolulu had 275, and New Orleans had 302 rapes in 1992. In relationship to their respective state populations, since state populations may render a broader picture of state activities, the forcible rape rate per 100,000 inhabitants is as follows: 66.0 Nevada, 51.7 Florida, 33.0 Hawaii, 40.9 Louisiana. It is clear that rape is a crime out of control in Nevada, and Nevada permits prostitution.

On the other hand, all four cities in reality have prostitutes. Legalized prostitution is not the issue. In Las Vegas, like Miami, Honolulu, and New Orleans, the degradation of women through advertisements is constant, yet it's clearly part of what makes Las Vegas what it is. Accordingly, its forcible rape rate is higher than Miami, Honolulu, and New Orleans, cities where tourists are as common as prostitutes.

Legalizing prostitution would not deter serial rapists and might increase first time offenders by marketing women's bodies the way Burger King markets burgers. It should be noted that the general crime index in Miami, Honolulu, and New Orleans was greater than Las Vegas, but forcible rape was the crime of choice in Las Vegas. One explanation could be that buying sexual contact through prostitution and forcing women into sexual contact are different activities. There is more to predatory rape than sexual contact. Rape could be a physiological and/or a psychological addiction.

Myth Four:
Since Criminals Disrespect Law and Order, They Commit Crimes

Criminal justice advocates might assert that criminals do not respect law and order and, therefore, commit crimes. However, a public opinion poll conducted by the General Social Surveys in 1972 in which 27,782 interviews were conducted by the National Opinion Research Center asked how much respect they had for the police in their area? Their responses showed that 77% said a great deal, 17% said some, 4% selected very little as their answer, and 2% claimed they don't know. In 1992, when people were asked the same question by the same organization, 60% said a great deal, 32% said some, 7% responded with hardly any and 1% weren't sure how much they respected law enforcement.

In general, public opinion of the police is low. Also, when the public was asked how they would rate the police in their community as to being helpful and friendly, 29% of the sample said excellent, 45% said pretty good, 19% said only fair, 6% poor, and the balance weren't sure or refused to respond. Additionally, when asked, about police and crime prevention, 16% said excellent, 42% pretty good, 28% only fair, 13% poor, and 1% weren't sure. Criminals might have low opinions of law enforcement, but so does everyone else. It is safe to assume that Americans see little relationship between law enforcement and crime control. If they did, maybe they would buy fewer guns and install fewer security systems.

Myth Five:
More Money and More Cops Means Greater Crime Control

Law enforcement supporters claim that more cops would mean fewer criminals. They say that huge increases in public funding could result in more officers and would make a stand for truth, justice, the American way. Is there a relationship between number of cops, operating costs, and crime? If law enforcement advocates are right, then forcible rape counts and total crime index rates would decrease as more money is spent. Each year, aside from a typical cost of living increase, as more money is spent to control crime, rape, and other criminally intense crimes should be affected.

In 1970, there were 534,537 state employees working in law enforcement with an operating cost of $6,026,948,000. In 1990, the U.S. Department of Justice reveals that there were 793,020 state employees working in law enforcement in 16,961 police agencies of all types at an operating cost of $41,550,270,000 across the United States. That is an increase of 48% (258,483) more people working in law enforcement with an increase cost of 589% ($35,523,332).

The Violent Crime Index shows 363.5 per 100,000 inhabitants in 1970 to 758.1 per 100,000 inhabitants in 1991 or an increase of 394.6 per 100,000 inhabitants. Therefore, in 20 years, crime per capita had increased by 108%. In the same period of time, forcible rape went from 7.9 to 42.3 per 100,000 inhabitants or an increase of 435%. As well, 258,000 more persons earned a pay check in law enforcement which amounted to a cost increase of 589% in expenses.

Can law enforcement with its current operating procedures control crime, especially violent crime? Or more specifically, how afraid are serial rapists of being apprehended by the police?[4] Serial rapists are more afraid of women who fight when attacked more than of being arrested. There were more uncompleted attempts of rape due to self protection measures employed by victims of rape (35,280 without the aid of a gun or a badge) than there were rape arrests in 1991 (40,120 arrests for all types of rape at a cost that stagers the imagination). Neither money nor number of law enforcement officers control or affect the Total Crime Index. Then, too, more officers might mean more specialization (a greater division of labor) rather than upgrading the training (and payroll) of the officers we already have. One study suggests that officers score low on job satisfaction scales and the source of their dissatisfaction is distrust of management and the public, diminished crime control discretion, and inadequate training programs.[5]

Myth Six:
Violent Crime is Declining

Myth Six claims that violent crime is declining in the United States. I've encountered this perspective often. The headline of a major newspaper read, "Who Says Crime Is Up?" The article detailed how the National Crime Victimization Survey is the best measure of crime trends. The message its numbers tell was heartening and contrary to conventional crime wave wisdom. Specially, the reporter showed that all crimes had declined by 6% since 1973. Household crime crimes were down by 3% and personal theft by 18%. The writer said that the actual number of unreported crimes through victimization reports had increased by 24% over the past 20 years. The article reflected the wisdom of Dr. George Cole, a political scientist at the University of Connecticut, who claimed that only 39% of all crime in 1992 had been reported to police. Therefore, the 2.5 million violent crimes reported to the police were really 61% greater as indicated by the unreported crimes. However, Cole argued that according to the National Crime Victimization Survey, a collection of 166,000 interviews showed that the rate of crimes was consistently in decline over the last decade.

Some prominent police advocates proclaimed that a police state will control crime and a Readers Digest senior editor, Eugene Methvin agreed with them. The first thing I tell my students is to scrutinize statistical sources. When something seems right, it's probably wrong. For example, the Total Crime Index showed that at a rate of 100,000 inhabitants in 1991 there were 5,897.8 crimes known to police. Looking through the years up to 1980, it showed 5,950.0 crimes which represented more crime. Therefore, I could argue one point of view or if I desired to argue something different, I could present the figures from 1987 showing less crime per capita or 5,540.0 per 100,000 inhabitants. Should those figures not say what I want to say, I could offer Criminal Victimization statistics or per capita calculations.' Then, too, by using 1981 victimization reports, a peak crime year, there is a decline for many crimes, but if we referenced another year and compare that year to 1991 or 1992 we'll show a decline.

Victimization reports compared with police reports for specific years for specific crimes show different conclusions. too. In 1973 49% of the rape victims reported the crime to police as compared with 41% in 1980, many more in 1981 (maybe that's why it was a peak crime year), and 59% reported rape in 1991. Also, in 1965 12.3 rapes were reported to the police per 100,000 of American inhabitants. In 1975, rapes rose to 26.3, in 1985 to 37.1, and in 1991 to 42.3 per 100,000 of our population. Additionally, there were almost 2,000,000 violent crimes committed suggesting that 758 individuals for every 100,000 people were victimized.

However, in the peak crime year of 1981, 6.6 million violent victimizations were reported while in 1991. 6.4 million were reported. Saying all crime is down because specific crimes are down is misleading. In every major city across the United States, murder and forcible rape rates are jumping higher than each preceding year over the past 20 years. However crime statistics are manipulated. or how careless an argument might sound in the grasp of a statistical computation, the fact remains that at no time in American history are females more likely to become forcible rape victims than now. The American public relies less on legal protection and more on defending itself as evidenced by the record number of firearms purchased and the number of women who take the law into their own hands. More guns mean less crime is committed, and it might follow that there would be less crime reported.

Myth Seven:
If We Lock Up Criminals, Rape Will Be Deterred.

That the threat of prison will deter criminals from committing predatory rape is argued by many supporters who believe that incarceration reduces criminally violent activities. If the threat of prison worked, every time a felon was incarcerated, crime should be affected. In 1971, BJS reported that there were 177,113 men and women incarcerated in state prisons across the United States at an annual cost of $2,289,058,000. There were another 160,863 individuals in municipal and county jails. There were also 57,239 juveniles in detention facilities that year. Altogether, there were 395,215 men, women, and children in state custody.[6]

In 1991, 20 years later, there were 711,643 inmates, plus another 424,000 men and women in jail. Additionally, there were 66,132 juveniles in public and private detention facilities. The above totals suggest that there were 1,201,775 men, women, and children in custody. The total cost for state and local institutional confinement was $19,954,487,000 excluding probation and parole expenses. This means that confinement increased by 806,560 individuals or an increase of 204% while expenses increased by $17.665,429,000 or 771%.[7] By June 30, 1993 BJS showed another huge increase in the prison population totaling 925,247 inmates in both state and federal penitentiaries.

Violent crime has been affected—it has gone up. In 1991, violence jumped from 396.0 per 100,000 inhabitants to 758.1 for an increase of 362.1 per 100,000 inhabitants or 91%. In particular, forcible rape was up from 8.6 per 100,000 to 42.3 or 391%. The main point is that confinement does not deter violent crime. When we consider it costs more to confine a criminal (which might not control crime) than to educate a child, something is wrong.

Another point about prison sentences is that when convicted criminals such as serial rapists are sent to prison, they continue to commit crime. it's simply not reported and when it is reported, it's ignored by officials.[8] Crime is supposedly reduced on the streets, but the habitual offenders have simply changed from one location where crime is more likely to be reported to another location where reporting is less likely. Serial rapists have changed their address, not their activities. When these criminals are released their raping sprees of innocent individuals continue.

The behavior of criminals places them outside of community's care, and it's the criminal justice system that is responsible for their welfare. But are we, the general population, victims by the very system designed to protect us? Like law enforcement, corrections. too. has tricked us into believing that the criminal justice system works for the good of law-abiding people and its clients, the criminals.

Time and again researchers find that the threat of prison time does not deter crime, especially violent crimes like serial rape. For example, in my own research at some of the toughest prisons in the United States—Attica in New York State and Stateville near Chicago, I learned that the criminal justice system perpetuates criminal activity by fueling anger through an ineffective, exploitative system of incarceration. Many others know that too. Why isn't something done about it? Students often ask, "Since these things are known, then how come policy doesn't change?" I respond, "In order for the criminal justice system to succeed, it seems as if it must fail.[9] It is highly unlikely that the most competent law enforcement officer or correctional officer performs adequately in every situation.[10] Therefore. many offenders including serial rapists are at-large. Correctional institutions fail to rehabilitate treatable inmates and that's one reason many are returned once released.[11] And the courts fail to prosecute known criminals due to insufficiency of evidence and triviality of the offense, although many of those cases dropped relate to assault and rape.[12] Therefore many career criminals such as serial rapists are free to engage in more crime. All in all, the system stays busy and builds more prisons, hires more cops, and prosecutes more criminals, but crime remains out of control."

[1] For more information see Seligman (1975). Then, too, the attributional model of learned helplessness (Abramson, Seligman, & Teasdale, 1978) might be more applicable to rape victims. Learned helplessness begins with the perception that we can't control something important. The more we explain this lack of control in terms of internal, stable, and global attributions. the more likely we are to feel helpless and depressed.

[2] See Brownmiller, 1975; Burgess & Holmstrom, 1974; Ellis, 1989; Groth, 1979; Groth & Burgess, 1980; Storaska, 1975.

[3] See Gordon & Riger (1989).

[4] High-risk offenders who have been apprehended for crimes of violence say that the threat of prison is not a deterrence of crime. Some criminals use the system as a way to enhance their own reputations. See Stevens (1992a). Also, high-risk offenders who had committed and were apprehended for heinous crimes of violence believe in capital punishment. The fact is that most career criminals have their own hard line notions of justice which do not include a court of appeal, plea bargaining, or reprieves. See Stevens (1992b)

[5] It is highly unlikely that the most competent officer performs adequately in every situation. Also, since most officers fail to see their experiences within the context of a social structure. that study perceives that alienation is caused by the institutional contradictions of law and order. Recommendations are that police administrations should manage through values instead of regulation, increase educational requirements for candidates, and employment raises and promotions linked to both education and experience (Stevens, 1998d). Therefore, it is unlikely that more cops will not necessarily solve the above problems but in fact, add to those problems.

[6] There were another 12,369 inmates in federal custody, but those statistics are unrelated to this discussion.

[7] For the record there were also 64,000 inmates in federal prisons.

[8] For a closer look see Eichental & Jacobs (1991).

[9] See Reiman (1995). Specifically. he suggests the term Pyrrhic Victory theory which is a military victory purchased at such a cost in troops and treasure that it amounts to a defeat. The Pyrrhic Victory theory argues that the failure of the criminal justice system yields such benefits to those in positions of power that it amount to success (p. 4). His discussion is so compelling that I have made his book required reading for my students at the university level.

[10] Police officers score low on job satisfaction scales, and the source of their dissatisfaction is seen as a distrust of the management who lead them and the public who bleeds them. discretionary powers dwarfed by mountains of redundant reform, and training programs incompatible with realities of the twenty-first century. Largely. law enforcement officers believe that their police departments are failing in their mission of law and order. and that officers do not control the streets of their community. For more detail see Stevens (1998d). Then, too, other evidence supports the postulation that the longer individuals work as correctional officers, the more likely they will become dissatisfied with their jobs. The

working correctional officer no longer controls the machinery of custody, but is controlled by it (Stevens, 1998I). My study showed that most correctional officers blame prison supervisors and department administrators for the failure of the prison to meet its organizational mission of custody and blame themselves for their frustration and anger.

[11] To examine the effects of time served and custody level on inmate attitudes and future anticipation of crime, I studied several prison populations and found that prisons themselves do not deter future crime, but promote it. For a closer look at male prisoners and future recidivism see Stevens (1995b; 1994b). For a closer look at female prisoners and future recidivism see Stevens (1998c).

[12] It turns out that the vast majority of all felony cases dropped by the prosecutor are rejected because of insufficiency of evidence—the police fail to produce adequate physical evidence or testimonial evidence from victims or eyewitnesses, argues Brian Frost (1995). However, one idea offered by narcotic officers to increase their arrest-conviction rates was adequately trained prosecutors who understood drug control techniques (see Stevens, 1998h).

CHAPTER THREE

RIVAL CAUSES OF SERIAL RAPE

An Overview: The Causes of Serial Rape

Official guidelines say that serial rape is described as vaginal and anal penetration, cunnilingus, ejaculation, and fellatio; therefore, sexual offenders exhibiting those actions are classified as sexually dangerous. Nonetheless, a great deal of controversy continues about why men sexually assault strangers. This chapter will highlight a few of the major perspectives of the vast literature about the causes of serial rape as well as some of the limitations of those views.[1] This brief outline and criticism about those perspectives are adequate for this study, as it would be too exhausting to list and criticize them all. Hopefully, this outline will offer a little insight into the contradictory study of serial rape.

Social Role Inequalities and Cultural Perspectives

Since antiquity, popular writers argue that the motivation for rape is males wanting to keep females in their place. The "real" motive of rape, these advocates say, is to preserve sexual role inequality through violence.[2] Males, for example, use violence to rape in order to keep women in a subordinate role. Consistent with this view, is the thought that rape is used to keep women from gaining independence and autonomy, i.e., rape demonstrates that women are really the property of men. The predatory rapist is seen as one focused on interpersonal violence, male dominance and sexual separation. In addition, sexual violence is an indicator of contempt that men have for female qualities. Rape is part of a culture of male violence.[3]

Psychological Predisposition

Related to male domination and control motivators, some psychologists argue that psychological and emotional factors predispose a person to react to situational and life events with sexual violence.[4] They argue that there are three major patterns of behavior represented by rapists: power rape, anger rape, and sadistic rape, one being dominant in every instance. They conclude that there are few rapes where sex is the chief motivator. Sex is largely instrumental to the service of non-sexual needs. Using this psychological model of motivation, a rapist is a person who has serious psychological difficulties that hinder his relationship with others. In sadistic rape too, where the offender relishes physical harm to the victim, control is the primary motivating force for the offender. This type of rapist discharges his feelings of rejection and anger through sexual acting-out. This particular view was one that my students seemed anxious to hear about in the classroom as it confirms what the popular press says about the fear of rape perspectives offered earlier. In fact, when I ask university students about the causes of predatory rape, they respond with ideas about control and power.[9]

Biological Perspectives

Another group of experts suggests that the attitudes of rapists toward women may not be particularly unusual. They say that rapists display specific attitudes and behavioral patterns of sexual arousal as compared to non-sexual offenders. This view says that coercion by violence is itself sexually arousing. Apparently, motivation for rape has to do with personality flaws inherited at birth; these flaws became salient as an individual interacts with his or her environment. Rapists cross a theoretical point called the forced copulation threshold due to neurological activities that are intimately linked with the effects of sex hormones upon brain functioning. Specifically, DNA molecules substantially influence the basic blue print of serial rapists. Also, a major part of this argument includes the idea that criminals move beyond the forced copulation threshold more than other law-abiding males.[5]

Social Learning

The social learning theory of aggression is a psychological perspective that says people learn how to behave by modeling themselves after others whom they have the opportunity to observe.[6] Some social learning experts see rape as resulting from the joint influences of cultural and experiential factors mediated by attitudes, sex role scripts, and other thought processes that link physical aggression and sexuality in the minds of males.[7] The social learning theory of rape basically portrays rape as part of aggressive behavior toward women learned through four interrelated processes: (1) by imitating rape scenes and other acts of violence toward women, as one may see in real life or as depicted in the mass media; (2) by associating sexuality and violence as when viewing sex and violence repeatedly depicted in the same context; (3) by perpetuating various rape myth such as "no means yes," and "women secretly desire to be raped;" and (4) by desensitizing viewers to the pain, fear, and humiliation of sexual aggression.[8] Therefore, some rapists can have a genuine appetite for sex but are socially trained to use violence to show that they want to have sex. The actual technique in committing rape is learned through a social learning process. But, social learning perspectives have a tendency to be fatalistic since they suggest that individuals have little resistance to rape should they observe it, and learning is not always accomplished. Social learning theory seems inadequate in explaining serial rape.

Subculture

Subculture theorists review police reports of rapists and largely conclude that predatory rape is motivated by a subculture theory of violence. Individuals in a subculture of violence learn the techniques of serial rape from their environment.[9] If an individual is socialized in a ghetto the likelihood that he will engage in violent crime is greater than an individual who had not been socialized in a ghetto. Yet, subculture perspectives neglect to consider that many individuals who have been raised in affluence across America attack their children, beat their wives, and rape their friends, employers, and clients.

Summary

In summary, with many convincing theories about the causes of serial rape, it's hard to imagine that they are all correct. Many of these theories advocate specific methods of victim response to sexual attackers— submission. Maybe it's time to hear from individuals who have committed serial rape, the experts from experience, in order to better understand offender motive, victim avoidance, and crime control techniques.

[1] However, there are limits on my work that must be clear before generalizing the conclusions of this paper. For example, I examined only incarcerated offenders who were predominantly from the lower socioeconomic class, thus, I believe that the results are generalizable only to those individuals with similar characteristics. Also, I measured specifically serial rape explanations and argue that other types of rape, such as date rape, may have significantly different characteristics than serial rape. And lastly, my unique orientation as a researcher, teacher, and adviser of high risk felons and enforcement agencies and officers, might differently effect my judgements about offenders than other writers.

[2] See Brownmiller (1975) and Sanday (1981).

[3] Yet, refuting this view is data from pre-industrial societies that show the existence of rape-free cultures. There might be some truth here, but I wonder if it were socially appropriate for women in those societies to report serial rape or not, and what would have happened if they had? For more information see Schwendinger and Schwendinger (1983) who offer a radical view. They say that in a capitalist society, their explanation about rape includes a form of exploitation of the politically weaker sex since men have and want to retain dominance. Since law determines rape's parameters, and men control the law, men control the sexuality of women.

[4] Nicholas Groth (1979) offers the best discussion on this view.

[5] Of particular interest are the following authors: Denno (1990), Ellis (1989), and Eysenck and Gudjonsson (1989).

[6] For a comprehensive discussion on criminological theory see Schmalleger (1998). His work on criminology far surpasses most scholarly efforts in the criminal justice arena. Accordingly, I require my students to use his work in my criminology and criminal justice courses.

[7] Albert Bandura (1973) presents the strongest argument on social learning.

[8] Lee Ellis (1989) on pages 11-12.

[9] See Schmalleger (1998) for more detail on this perspective. However, the subculture of violence blames environmental conditions, which ultimately implicates, among other things, a lack of efficient law enforcement and parental control, and often furthers a victim precipitation perspective. For example, Menachem Amir (1971) studied rape police reports and argued that since victims were known to their offenders and many of them had been sexually active with their attackers, those victims played an important role in their own attack. Amir's perspective is dated. biased, and weakens offender accountability. It blames the victim for the crime of an offender.

CHAPTER FOUR

MOTIVES OF SERIAL RAPE: LUST, RIGHTEOUS, AND PEER RAPE

Motives of Serial Rapists in The Sample

When offender accounts were examined for motives leading to predatory attacks, clear patterns emerged: 42% (25) of the offenders largely characterized sexual contact or lust as their primary goal for attacking females (see Table 2)[1] Fifteen percent (9) of the offenders revealed that their predatory attacks were encouraged by the victims themselves or what the participants called "righteous rape." Three percent (2) of the offenders blamed friends or peers as their reasons for their attacks. Another 8% (5) of the offenders suggested control/anger as their motivating force bringing them to serial rape, while 13% (8) of the rapists described supremacy over their victims as their goal. Sixteen percent (10) of the participants described fantasy as the motivating force behind their attacks, and 3% (2) of the respondents presented unclear descriptions about their motivators. Because lust, righteous, and peer rapists are different in terms of motives, sexual goals, and violence, they are discussed in this chapter, and control/anger, supremacy, fantasy, and unclear motives are discussed in the preceding chapter.

Lust Rape Motives

Lust as an objective was described by many of the predatory rapists, and some of the offenders described lust as their only goal. Specifically, 42% (25) of the accounts described lustful characteristics. With lust as a primary goal, the statements of the participants were carefully examined for indicators of a sexual nature, selection techniques (Chapter 6), and use of force (Chapter 7). Some of the typical remarks leading to this conclusion include the following.

> I watched her ass... and I watched her eyes... I got this chill running down my legs to the accelerator (of my car). Henry

> Watching this cunt walk at the pool stoked my insides. An itch the size of a horse licked my dick. John

> There was something about the way she looked. I wanted to see if she looked the same way when her ol'e man was humping her. Barry

> It's simple, man, I love pussy. Carmen

Account after account suggested that licentiously driven offenders had time prior to their attacks to make conscious assessments about their victims. That is, the gauges used to determine lust as a primary motive included both statements of a sexual nature and indications that offenders had opportunities to make assessments of the victims prior to their attacks. For example:

> The ol'e guy saw me and I was polite. I helped them into the elevator and touched her tits and ass while holding her up. Not bad, I remember thinking. I decided I'd screw her if I could..... He passed out in the living room. and I poured her into bed. I think she pushed me away, but I held her hands with one hand and pulled her skirt up. Her cunt smelled, but it welcomed my dick and it seemed forever but I finally came [ejaculated]. He suddenly appeared and started hitting me. I shoved him. He kept on com en. When I ran out. I forgot my shoes. Stephen

> I was watching this babe peddling her bike. She looks good, and I was hungry. She's real young. I wanted that cunt. I knew she couldn't stop me. I ran along and ask if she saw my little sis. She stops, and I smell her sweat. I wan'na taste it. We walked together talk'en 'bout my sis till we passed a field. So I took that little babe and made her chew my dick. That was it for me... I pulled them shorts down and god, was she wet. It slid in deep like Grant took Richmond. Billy

This tight look'en girl was fumbling with her keys, tr'en to get into her fal'en down shed [in her yard]. I saw her from the street. She wore a nightee that I could almost see (her) through. The way she moved made my rocks shake. I had to have her. So I pretended to look for my dog. She was much older than I thought. She like was polite but bitchy... Told her som'en like, sorry lady. She goes, yea like get lost. Now I don't give a fuck, ya know. I reach for her neck. Fuck you, I goes, and drag her inside the fuc'en shed. Okay, now put your mouth on this or som'en like that, I goes. I was too fuc'en scared to get hard. ...okay, this babe goes, naa, fuck you man and spits on me. I ran. Cidel

Other descriptions characterized by lustful offenders which distinguished them from the other serial rapist categories were that their descriptions often revealed a preference for vaginal penetration. They used vulgar adjectives to describe victims less often than the other rapists; and they were intense men who characterized emotional feelings for their victims. Some of those emotional-charged comments came before their sexual attack and some came after it. For example:

One time this honey was asleep but I just looked till I...[2]

[after the attack] ...kissed her. Robby

Be still... held her like aaa... liked that sexy creature for a moment.

But she [the victim] made me so horny, I went home and screwed my ol'e lady to death. I member... something though... screw'en my ol'e lady... I 'membered that little babe's eyes. They were mmm. pretties real pretties and gentle like. Collin

Lust is not a new idea concerning predatory rape, yet most writers who suggest it as a motivator say it is a secondary goal. As evidenced by the above descriptions, many predatory rapists are driven by their desire to have immediate sexual contact with females. They most often prefer sexual intercourse with their victims, desire ejaculation inside her body (as opposed to outside her body), and they are often emotionally involved with their prey. It should be noted that lustful offenders' victim selection techniques were more focused on easy-prey techniques as explained in Chapter 6, and they rarely used force to subdue their victims before, during, or after their sexual attacks as explained in more detail in Chapter 7.

Righteous Rape Motives

Of 61 predatory rape cases, 15% (9) of the descriptions characterized what those rapists called righteous rape as a primary motive for their attacks. These nine offenders said that their victims produced "the circumstances and the conditions" for rape by striking a "silent deal" with them as one rapist explained it. That is, some predators (and defense lawyers) often blamed victims for the attacks.

From the perspective of an offender, it's easier to blame someone else for the crimes he committed than himself. That way, an offender doesn't sound as bad as his behavior looks nor does he have to accept the responsibility for his actions. Why not tag a person he already knows is an easy target? In fact, most of these offenders distinguished their motives from the other categories of motives through their use of easy-prey target techniques as discussed in Chapter 6 . They also thought of themselves as predators who used little if any physical force before, during, or after their attack as discussed in Chapter 7. This type of thinking is found in Wild Bill's following statement.

> I was mind'en my own friggen business, do'en some real good shit
> [drugs] near the swings, when this sweet white babe shots her parts
> my's way and smiles. Ya give me some blow [drugs], and I'll show
> ya a good time. she says.

As far as Wild Bill saw it, she made a deal with him. Maybe she did, but part of the deal certainly didn't include rape. Wild Bill felt that he was an innocent bystander. As Wild Bill presented more of his story, he revealed his true mission.

> She looks good, real nice. See, man, I wants this 'hole, so I let her help herself. She did'em and walks, laughing -- telling (her) friends she made me. I catch her later on a back street and lay the 'hole down. I goes som'en like you owe. She don't act nothing like she's expecting it. I knew she'd be sweet. How'd I know tat' hole was twelve! But I had the right to that snatch. She gets exactly what she asks for, my big dick. Wild Bill

These offenders are saying is an attempting to justify both their method of coercion and the sexual attack itself. They are not guilty by reason of circumstance. It seems that righteous rape accounts could easily fit the lustful rape motive accounts as Wild Bill's aim is directed towards sexual contact. He's done this before and knows the game. Blaming a victim isn't the cause of the attack.

There is one major differences in the accounts of the righteous rapists and the accounts of lustful rapists; in the righteous cases, unlike the lustful rapists, they seem to justify their attacks. For example:

> I got drunk one night with this piece of shit bitch I worked with. We started making it in her car. I went down on her and she touched me like she enjoyed it. She got me so frigg'en hard that I'd have a stroke if she didn't make me come. I told her she'd better suck me off or else. Fuck it, I said. I was horny, I just pushed it into her bitch-pit and came as I did. It was fuck'en what's happen'n man... Hampton

> I believe it's clear where Ben is going with his remarks by suggesting that she enjoyed their sexual activity. He is inferring that his victim is now obligated to go as far as he wanted her too. Notice, I'm saying as far as he wanted her to go! Yet, as Ben continues his narrative, he reports that he knew his attack was rape, but he solicits sympathy trying to sell someone on the idea he became a victim of both the victim and the state. Narration presented by the inmate-interviewee.

Blaming rape victims for rape suggests an awareness of cultural ideal that rape is an inappropriate sexual activity. Rape is a cultural deviance. Therefore, in order to be a conformist, or one of the good guys, a rapist must place the blame on others. To say I attacked a woman because I wanted to have sex with her might be the comment of a man who doesn't care what others think or an offender who is not up for parole. Righteous rapists apparently care what others think, right down to their method of their sexual assault.

Then too, some psychologists like to dig into a rapist's past and explain the blame from those experiences of an offender.[10] The truth of the matter is as one of the rapists said about most of the women he attacked, "She was so sexy! I couldn't stop. I'd eat her shit to fuck her every day—every way, man." Because his victims were attractive, it follows that it was her fault that he raped her. Why didn't he date her or court her or marry her in order to have sex with her since Marvin, like the other righteous rapists, claimed that he would do anything to have sex with his victims? In what way might Marvin's early childhood experiences have something to do with his behavior 20 some years later? The unique thing about humans is that they are constantly changing. Humans evaluate and re-evaluate their social environments, ideals, and experiences all the time. Most of us develop our own social meanings and social realities. What was true yesterday, isn't necessarily true today. Our divorce rate also exemplifies this desire to change. Yet human behavior is goal driven.[3] Many children have had abusive experiences and they aren't raping and killing.

In sum, both lustful and righteous offenders characterized sexual intimacy as their primary objective for their predatory attacks. They individually and collectively described similar methods of finding and subduing their victims (see Chapters 6 & 7), and preferred sexual intercourse with their victims but the righteous rapists also sought oral sex.

Peer Rape Motives

Oddly enough, 3% (2) of the offenders' accounts characterized friendship as a cause for rape. "I had no choice, I ran with bad company," Tyrone said. Righteous rapists blamed victims, peer rapists blamed friends for criminality. For instance:

Michael is a 24-year-old black male serving a sentence of 28 years for his participation in a gang rape which took place in 1987. Michael admits his participation but pled not guilty, and maintains he is without responsibility for the incident stating that he was forced into it by two co-defendants. He indicated his co-defendants questioned his masculinity and called him chicken as well as threatened him with physical violence. He had to prove himself. They were at the playground and decided on a 13 year old who liked to hang with them and they thought she was some kind'a groupie. One of the inmate-interviewer reported.

Bernard and his partner went camping. A woman was hiking along the trail. Bernard's friend told him that this was the opportunity he was waiting for. He grabbed the woman. He tore off her clothes and told him to take his off. Then he forced her into oral sex with Bernard. When Bernard hesitated, he called him chicken shit. Bernard noticed that his partner was not hard, but had sex with her anyway. She was skinny and didn't turn Bernard on. He was shaking and afraid of getting caught. His partner whispered that we should kill her. Bernard said no. Having a partner is like being drunk, you feel braver and stronger. An inmate-interviewer reported.

Explaining peer motives is similar to the above discussion about righteous rapists, except in peer rape an offender blames his partner and in righteous rape an offender blames his victim. The excuses of both peer rapists and righteous rapists are designed to relieve these offenders of their criminal responsibility and justify their conduct and any consequences arising from that conduct.[4] In fact, some offenders think they should not be punished for rape because they hadn't committed a crime. This reminds me of the prostitute who thinks she's a social worker or the drug pusher who thinks he's altruistic. I think responses like these

44

are an attempt to defend inappropriate conduct. My first point is that this offender knows his behavior was criminal, and secondly the explanation he is giving about his crime is fixed in his current experiences rather than his past experiences.[5] Righteous rapists and peer rapists are using present experiences to explain historical accounts. It could be that they think it fashionable to blame their victims for their crimes.

Table 2   Rape Motive Categories*   (N=61)

Category	Percent	Number
Lust	42%	25
Righteous	15%	9
Peer	3%	2
Control/Anger	8%	5
Supremacy	13%	8
Fantasy	16%	10
Unclear	3%	2
Total	100%	61

* percents rounded therefore column does not equal 100%

[1] Other researchers also find that a strong desire for sexual intimacy can lead to stranger rape among certain men, however, none of these writers argue that sexual intimacy is the primary motive for most predatory rapists (Felson & Krohn, 1990; Hazelwood & Warren, 1990; MacKinnon, 1987; Scully, 1990).
[2] When the lustful offenders spoke about their victims before and many times after their attacks, they distinguished their victims as: honeys, babes, sweet things, cute, sexy creatures, dolls, young sweeties, killer babes, lovelies, and pretties. That is, they referred to females as objects of endearment and rarely used vulgar adjectives to describe them.
[3] When our goals seem unchanging, other variables or factors might be responsible. For example, a cigarette smoker who tries to change his or her smoking habit finds it difficult due to psychological and physiological dependence.
[4] For an in-depth look at this discussion see Stanford Lyman and Marvin Scott (1989).

[5]For example, in a study of 419 inmates at Attica penitentiary in New York, one finding arising from the data was that offenders idealize their attitudinal beliefs couched in present experiences. Also, those idealized versions of themselves possessed a different meaning than the meaning noted by some experts who assessed offenders because many experts share in a different set of experiences than apprehended criminals. For example, in that study most of the chronic offenders said that waiting is beneficial. To some experts, waiting might denote that predators are doing their time—waiting to be released. Is it possible that they are waiting to end the questionnaire and/or are waiting for their next victim in prison? See Stevens (1997c). Also, see C. Wright Mills (1940; 1951).

CHAPTER FIVE

MOTIVES OF SERIAL RAPE: CONTROL/ANGER, SUPREMACY, FANTASY RAPE, AND UNCLEAR

Control and Anger Rape Motives

Eight percent (6) of the accounts characterized control and anger as a primary motive leading to serial rape. In these accounts, the offenders described more violence than necessary to accomplish rape. Violence was used even after the victim submitted and during the entire encounter, illustrating the use of violence for its own sake. These individuals who pursued violence reported great degrees of anger as well. The rapes were described as secondary to the violence powered by their anger. For example:

> I was pissed with my wife... looking for action. But I didn't wan'a fuck, and I didn't want to hear screams. So, if I found some bitch who was dead or unconscious even, hypothetically that is, then she can't scream and sure as hell can't say no like my frigg'en wife. I saw this fine looking broad in the parking lot carrying a load of food with a little kid hanging on to her dress. I pushed her into the car and grabbed the kid by the throat. I slid in on top of her and said to the bitch, if you ain't a good little girl, I'd kill your kid. She said something to me that I didn't understand so I slammed the shit out of her with my free hand. I told her, I want you to suck my cock. She started to but the kid won't shut up so I shook it. And she was crying really loud. I ran. Jake. Note: never arrested for this crime.

Control and anger seem to flow from each word Jake offered. But Jake tended to describe a minimal amount of force in comparison to Bones who offered a typical control and anger perspective.

I picked up this chick at some rat hole [bar]. We got in my car and started petting and petting. She stopped; said she should'a been with her husband. Imagine, she's go'en down (oral sex) on me and now I'm not good enough for her. Fuck her! I pulled her hair almost off her skull and shove my beer bottle in her pussy as far as it could go. You should'a seen her face, when I pulled her out of the car with her hair in one hand and the bottle in t'a other! She found out who was in charge, and it ain't her. I pulled the bottle out of her cunt and slammed her a homer [rape] while I held her by the hair. I think she was off the ground the whole time. She was sort of not with it. but I made her finish me off in her mouth. Bones. Note: never arrested for this crime

Control and anger seem to be related variables in these narratives. sexuality is only the means of expressing the aggressive needs and feelings that operate in the offender and underline his assault. These rapists are different from those in the previous chapter (lust, righteous, and peer) not only in terms of motives but also in sexual goals. For control and anger rapists oral sex was preferred, ejaculation could be anywhere outside the body of the victim. Violence too was more pronounced, and degradation of the victims was more apparent. Sexual contact seems to have been a secondary goal for them.

Supremacy Rape Motives

Thirteen percent (8) of the participants described their forcible rape attacks with an emphasis upon unnecessary violence before, during, and after the attack. I refer to these individuals as supremacy rapists. These respondents characterized anger as rage to gain victim submission. Sadly, their rage continued long past victim subjugation and in some cases long past a victim's demise. Rage blinds their violence and sex is their alibi to exercise it. They seem to have little interest in sex itself as evidenced by the Jerry's example:

Me and a lot of other kids were in this temporary foster house for abused kids. The daughter of the house-parents was always bossing us around, so one day that was it! I threw her on the bed. We fought for a while. I won. And put it to that little fucken whore. After that I forced into sex when ever I had noth'en to do and made her come up to my room to spend the night... I told her I'd tell her parents that she was screw'en all of us and would get pregnant if she told. A few times I forced her to have oral sex with some of the other guys. I think she was like 10. This went on a few weeks till they found me a foster home. I showed the little bitch 'bout sex. Got their dog up stairs once and made her watch when I made the little fucker shot its wad by pulling its meat. She said she liked it. I told her if she said anything that that dog was gonna hump her and then bite her friggen nipples. Jerry

Sexual contact played an insignificant role; what took precedence for this rapist was the punishment he inflicted on his victims. This rapist demonstrated little regard for his victim as a human being. They transcend humanity especially the humanity of their victims. Their victims were punching bags designed to absorb their rage and their urges. Manny's descriptions of predatory rape below revealed each of these characteristics and brought to light other characteristics of the supremacy rapist:

I followed her to her car. I looked like I was getting in the car next to hers checking everything out. When she opened her door... was busy being it was Christmas time, I pushed inside and forced her to the floor. She was cry'en so I kicked her and told her to shut the fuck up. Bout a mile out of town I pulled into a abandoned lot. I grabbed her by the hair. You suck this bitch... She must'a been afraid cuz she crapped right there. Fuck'en aaaa, man. I rubbed her fuck'en face in it like the fuck'en whore dog she is. Drove around town for awhile; She didn't run or cry or nothin'. At McDonalds, I told her to go down on me but the fuck'en shit smelled, man... finally said screw it, and put it in her right there in the lot but covered her face with her skirt. She was cold the whole time. I pissed on her. ...kept some of her I.D. and spent all her money. I told her that if she fingers me. I'd get her... Drove by the cunt's house and watched... Kept that bitch the rest of the night... punched her ass... Driving down the friggen highway (interstate), she passed out from the shit I was push'en down her throat (drugs and liquor); that's when I did it (pushed her out on to the interstate). Sam

Closer inspection of the above accounts suggests that supremacy rapists used sex as a devise to inflict degradation and punishment on their victims. Individuals who commit the crime of rape do so in an effort to deal with the unresolved and the conflicted aspects of their lives. Supremacy rape is an expression of power and assertion of the rapist's strength and manhood. These rapists are people who have taken woman hating to its furthest possible point— the actual acting out of the body that some men do only in fantasy.[1]

Fantasy Rape Motives

Sixteen percent (10) of the accounts suggested that the respondents were attempting to fulfill imaginary goals reflecting unreality or invented scenarios. These individuals were primarily trying to regain some imaginary goal that had been part of their past. Sexual contact was described as an event that helped fulfill that goal. Sex may not have been a goal and in many cases, unnecessary. For example, Martin said:

> In my head I think about women in precarious positions. I devise shit like spreading her legs on a rack. I think about hurting'em and tak'en in their cries for help. But, I don't do any of that shit. I tell'em once — okay, bitch you know what I want. This could go hard or easy on you. It's up to you. Most of the time, they put out that fast and usual say shit like, don't kill me. Please, don't kill me! Hell, I don't want'a kill'em, I just want'a screw'em. Martin

Martin conveyed that he was motivated by his ideas that he had created. However, other accounts described more than visions and characterized behavior showing how the participant turned his thoughts into criminally violent behavior to fulfill his objectives. For instance, Henry, in the following account, explained his illusion:

> When I was little, my uncle used to baby sit me. I used to spy on him and his girl friend when they had sex. The way they went through the motions was perfect. I wanted to be just like them. Henry

However, as Henry revealed more of his experiences, his thoughts led to behavior suggesting that he was attempting to bring those illusions to reality.

> So when I was with girls I pretend I was him (his uncle) and they were her. I'd tell'em how I wanted them to lay or form their body. I'd masturbate on'em. When I was a punk, I d break into homes and force old fuck'en folks there into venous positions and masturbate. Sometimes... I pretended I was my uncle's slut. I made sure some of those folks pulled their chains (masturbated) on me. Henry

Unfortunately, the behavior described by Henry took violent turns. Henry wanted to pursue his goal no matter the cost as the benefits of his deed far outweighed the consequences of his crime. It seems that all serial rapists weigh the benefits of their crimes and not the consequences of their behavior.[2] Apparently, criminals like the those described above have a definable plan which brings to mind offenders such as Edward Gein who danced in the moonlight wearing the face, the breasts, and the vaginas of his victims.[3]

Unclear Rape Motives

Unclear motives were suggested by 3 percent (2) of the participants. However, the example below seems to complement a power perspective and/or a cultural inequality view.

> My guy says he sees a chick in the parking lot that he knows will love his ass once they're together. Inside, he goes up to her and if she owns a certain car and gives her the tag (license plate) number. He says that

these babes always sound like they're doing him a favor by talking to him, but he always has a upper hand because he's smarter. He describes something on the seat, and asks about the small animal socked inside that looks sick. She runs to the car. Inside looking for the cat, she goes, I own your ass, bitch. You can get hurt or it will be over soon. He sat on her chess and pulls his meat (masturbates) in her face. He wants to start quick and end quickly. When he shoots, it goes in her mouth. He splits. An interviewer explained.

The account does suggest that there were lustful intentions on the part of the rapist.

Summary

In summary, from this and the previous chapter the data suggest that 62 percent (38) of the respondents (lust, righteous rape, peer, and unclear) characterized lustful intentions as their primary goal leading to their sexual attacks. For some their lust led them to believe that their victims promoted the circumstances and the conditions for rape. In this chapter, the data show that offenders raped in order to gain control over their victims and other offenders raped for total domination over their victims. Then, too, some of the descriptions of the rapists characterized fantasy rape that was fueled by lustful imaginations.

Some experts say that most predatory rapists are violent and angry men, and I think we can see from the above statements typifying violent offenders that they offer some valuable insight. Yet they fail to recognize that many men are angry, and many men have reason to be angry with many experiences including their experiences with women. What also comes to light is that the rage of some these rapists is tied directly to their string of conscious decisions as they move toward their primary objective—sex and dominance. Control might be the best way of explaining their actions. Are they in control of their own rage? Can they turn it off and can they turn it on? In a word, yes. Emotions such as anger and rage are devices used by some offenders to manipulate others support this idea.[4]

Some descriptions of violent men are inadequate especially when they show that some deep-seated mysterious mechanism triggers these men into action. The actions described by the rapists in this study did not support any idea that their actions were tied to some mysterious source.

No single pattern of rape represents all serial rapists. Many people visualize rape in the form of a sex-starved madman waiting with a weapon for his prey. Despite the consistency in the stereotype, characterizing stranger rape requires diversity yet sexual contact seems to play an important role. There is no one type of stranger rapist just as there is no one type of stranger rape victim. Yet, most violent offenders like serial rapists, weigh the benefits of their crimes without considering the consequences arising from them. Most rapists can not be deterred from committing crimes of violence out of fear of apprehension, prison, or capital punishment.[5]

[1] Also, see Les Sussman and Sally Bordwell (1981).

[2] Also, see Gottfredson and Hirschi (1990) who hold a similar perspective about career criminals.

[3] For a closer look see Gollmar. R. H. (1981). Edward Gein. NY: Windsor Publishing.

[4] See Averill (1993) for more details on this idea.

[5] A study based on interviews with inmates at one of Chicago's highest risk prisons suggests that fear of apprehension and serving prison time does little to deter crime. And if confined, many inmates use prison to advance their own criminal reputations, once released. For more details see Stevens (1992b). Also, 307 inmates in some of the highest risk penitentiaries in Illinois and South Carolina reported similar perspectives about capital punishment as pubic opinion surveys conducted with free populations. That is, capital punishment is an appropriate punishment for criminals. However, the inmates reported that the threat of capital punishment was not a deterrent of violent crimes. The use of capital punishment actually increased crimes of violence since violent prone criminals identified with the executioner instead of the condemned criminal. See Stevens (1992a) for more detail.

CHAPTER SIX

VICTIM SELECTION TECHNIQUES

Victim Selection

Which females do predators attack most often? Attractive women? Young girls? Athletic females? When the answers of the chronic offenders were placed into categories to answer that question, the most frequently mentioned characteristic of victim selection wasn't looks or age but vulnerability. When predators thought a female could not or would not resist an attack and an opportunity prevailed by circumstance or manipulation, they attacked regardless of her appearance, age, or physical condition. The following categories[1] (see Table 3) arose from the data of the offenders: easy prey; random; situational; and unclear.

TABLE 3		TARGET SELECTION METHODS
(N=61)		
	NUMBER	PERCENTS
EASY PREY	42	69%
RANDOM	7	11%
SITUATIONAL	9	15%
NOT SURE	3	5%

Easy Prey

Forty-two of the 61 rapists (69%) characterized victim vulnerability in their descriptions as the best reason to sexually attack a female. They were easy

56

prey. Easy prey specifically refers to females whom the offenders perceived as vulnerable. "Hell, the easiest (prey) are the ones out of it or old, I mean old," said Kelly. Just how easy is easy? Below are two typical accounts describing how offenders selected there "out of it" or "old" victims to sexually attack.

> I was parking my car in the condo lot where I was renting. This older couple pulled in. They were drunk... Dwayne

> I was working maintenance at a hospital in Florida. I'd keep my eye on the women patients and every so often go into their rooms when they were out of it and screw'em. I got caught but said it happened only once. They didn't want the publicity so they fired me and never called the cops. I knew they'd do that cause it happened before at a old people's home where I worked. Hurbert (Note: never arrested or convicted for any sexual crime)

Young Girls as Easy Prey

There were disagreements between the participants about which females were easy prey. "The easiest (prey) is young girls," claimed Hank. The following is a typical narrative about victim selection:

> I stopped at this chain joint for lunch somewhere between Knoxville and Ashville. ...I ordered and this real cute girl caught my eye. She must'a been with her folks. Maybe she was 14, maybe 12. She saw me grin and smiled back. That's the tip off that I can have her. (When) she headed for the bathroom... Hank

Hank went into detail about his attack, an attack suggesting that if his victim was older or more experienced, things might have turned out different. Age and/or inexperience were determining factors. He continued with:

> I made a line for it (bathroom) too real slow like, look'en to the ground so not to cause no stir. She went in. I went in. Someone was in a stall, but no one was outside. She didn't say a word when I grabbed her arm. I frowned and went shhh, don't want to hurt ya, I says. I moved her into

the end stall. I guess I was scared cause I couldn't get in her. She was real dry and I was seat'en on the stool with her on my lap. The woman in the stall finished up. I pushed her to the floor and put it [his penis] in her mouth. Don't ya spit it out when I come, I said real low. And when I came, it leaked over her lips. Cleaned it off with toilet paper and kissed her. Hank

Another offender. Eddy, characterized how a younger or less experienced female became his victim once he determined her vulnerably.

Watching this shit-flick at the movies but watch'en these young sweeties a few rows down. Each time they leave, they're gone for 10 minutes or so. Probably screw'en around somewhere. When they leave, I waltz up next to the one they left behind. I smile but she doesn't look at me. I put my knife to her stomach. Put your mouth on it, I say tak'en my dick out of my pants. She hesitated but I push the knife into her more. She covers my dick and I could almost get off like that. Went into the john and yanked off in a stall watching these guys pee. Left that movie place and never went back. Eddy (Note: never prosecuted).

How can perceived vulnerability of children be related to easy prey? One explanation is that younger females demonstrate cues to predators through their behavior, in part, due to their caretakers who assume that their children are more responsible and mentally mature then they are. Many parents treat their children like friends and have adult expectations for them.[2]

A analysis of affluent middle class children shows that they tend to have more freedom than lower class children since their caretakers tend to ignore or pass to others (i.e. psychiatric hospitals or councilors) the essential discipline and guidance which children require to develop interpersonal skills to deal with predators.[3] Therefore, children tend to rely upon their limited experiences and unlimited choices when confronted by strangers believing that they are in control and that no harm will come to them. What some children fail to recognize is that they are no longer dealing with people who are accountable for their actions.

Additionally, as evidenced by Hank and Eddy's comments, predators know how to use childhood independence against their victims.

Middle Class Females as Easy Prey Victims

Women working in the financial and banking centers of large cities acquiescence to predators as well. For example, Randall, a 31 year old black man convicted of armed robbery (only one victim testified against him in a sexual misconduct charge), had "sixty or seventy naive women" who were his victims. Before incarceration, he regularly scouted the financial districts of several cities for sex and money. He would lean on his shiny late model Cadillac wearing an expensive suit. As a "hip well-dressed" woman walked by, he would smile and ask for information. He said that when a woman answered his question and "glances down or looks away," he knew she could be victimized. A friend of Randall claimed that lower class women would tell him to "go fuck himself and stare him down. But patty (white Irish] girls are trained to be polite, but look's away from a black buck like him."

Women tend to internalize messages that devalue femaleness from an early age suggesting that they are irrational, immoral, emotional, dependent, and submissive. These predators search for females who have been socially trained to yield to males once approached. Pleasant conversation is pursued and intimidation is used, if necessary, to frighten her into obedience if she does not at first comply with his sexual demands. Randall is a typical example of a rapist who rarely attacked females whom he perceives as street-wise.

Occupational Tracking and Easy Prey

Part of the ease of victims encountered in the streets by predators is due to the early childhood training of many middle class females who are too independent or, in this case, were socially trained as supportive individuals responding to the needs of others. Another part is due to occupational tracking of females into helper roles like nurses, teachers, and social workers. Submissive roles at home and in the work place are routinely demanded of females. Another way of explaining women's obedience is that predators manipulate "helping women" into vulnerable situations by drawing upon their helper objectives. For instance:

> Saw this doll alone run'en down the road. I watched her ass jump up and down before I passed her, and I watched her eyes squint through my mirror. I got this chill running down my legs to the accelerator. The next thing was, could it happen without a fight? I pulled my van on the side of the road and fiddled under the hood. Soon I saw her coming towards me. I put my knuckle on the manifold and burned the fuck out of'em. I screamed and she came a'run'en. I told her my first aid kit was in the glove box. She climbed in. That was it. Do it or else, I say. She didn't fuss or nothing. Edmond

> I follow some cute babe from the parking lot at a mall. ...I ask her bout the small animal locked in the car. ...it looks sick or something. We almost run to. Tyrone

In the role of helpers these women are easy prey.

Shoppers as Easy Prey

Other selection processes have to do with how a shopper "carries" herself, her demeanor. For instance, one rapist said he observed how women respond to others as shoppers at food stores. Women who bumped into other shoppers and were "overly apologetic, were dead give-aways." Other typical descriptions follow:

If she's not watching what's happening all around her, then doesn't know how to handle herself, how to use the things around her to hurt me or get me caught. Jona

Whether we're talk'en bout a robbery or sex, depends on the mark (victim]. See, if they're going to hurt me, no way. When these broads are awake (alert, they] tell ya to 'get bent' right out when ya approach'em. Brent

In sum, the nonverbal cues or messages a female sends apparently has much to do with how predators perceive her defense attitudes. "If she's dizzy say at K Mart's checkout, it means she probably won't make a decision to strike back till it's too late, if she's going to do it at all," claimed our food store predator. Nonverbal communication is often an honest mirror of the thoughts of human beings, and it adds a whole new dimension to the communication process. Apparently, chronic offenders rely on their skill of reading nonverbal cues as part of their decision-making process to attack or not to attack a victim. Unfortunately fear entrepreneurs both promote and reinforce the fear of rape and a learned helplessness among females. Females learn that they can not win against assailants. They simply follow the advice of those they trust and give in.

Females Who Decrease Their Defense Capabilities

Of course, predatory rapists do not always succeed. But the more they attack helpless "appearing" women, the greater their chance of success. "It's a numbers game," claimed Bubba. Women decrease their defense capabilities by placing themselves in dangerous situations—situations that do not go unnoticed. For instance:

I watched this old bitch at a party get high. I've seen her around campus a few times and was interested. She was messing with everybody. What a tease! I danced with her a few times and suggested we go into one of the bedrooms. Kiss'en, hug'en, touch'en, ya know the scene. When I was ready to do her, she goes, no man, not that. I'm married. Fuck you, I says. She pushed me away but she was so high she couldn't get up enough push. Bamm. I'm in her and at first she's struggling a little then she got in to it. Man, she shook her ass so much I thought I'd lose my dick in her. She called campus police in the morning and they asked me about it. I told'em what I'm telling you and they said she didn't have a case. I agree, the bitch! I ain't seen her around anymore. Her ol'e man probably made her drop out. Serves her right. Glen

In sum, 69% of the descriptions of the rapists characterized easy prey as their primary criterion prior to sexually attacking a female.

Random

Prior to any sexual attacks 7 (11%) of the offenders revealed that while they were engaged in another activity like robbery or criminal trespass, they came upon their victims by chance. In this sense, the offenders were not actively seeking victims. However, in most of the descriptions they suggested that almost immediately upon discovering a female, they altered their earlier activities and assaulted her. The following typical statements characterized the chance victim selection descriptions of the sample.

We broke into this hospital drug store... I ducked into a room where this chick is out cold. I saw in a movie where this guy gets in a hospital bed and when they check, they don't see nothing but the patient. So, in I go (under the covers with his victim). Emory

Each morn'en bout 9:00 to 12:00 when I'm on the move, I check motels out cause that's when the maids are clea'em up... I get lucky and find a key. Bout dinner time, I'd come back and chec'em out. I'd make people for small things. One time, this honey's asleep... Stinger

In these cases any female could have been victimized regardless of her appearance, age, or condition. Every female is a potential victim of a serial rapist if she happens to become part of his environment and he perceives her as vulnerable and/or manipulates her into submission through intimidation and/or violence. For example:

> One of my old partners told me that he broke into this beach house where this real young thing, probably 12 or 8, I don't know, was slee'en in just shorts. When she opened her eyes, she went wide-eyed. He told her som'em like everything's c'oo, just do as I say, and I'll leave. She pushed him and they rolled on the carpet. He thought, oh shit, he'd better split. Be still, he says and holds her like... he really liked that sexy creature for a moment. She said okay, but don't hurt me, mister. My friend said he turned her over, pulled her bottoms down, and greased her with the suntan lotion on the dresser and pushed his dick in her ass while he shoved his thumb up her little pussy. She bleed from every hole when he was done. Bart.

Random victimization suggests that the offender had no opportunity to assess his victim prior to raping her. All he knew was that she was a female and breathing. For example:

> We breaks a lock on a railroad car full of merchandise when two guards pops us with guns in the middle of the night. My partner kicks one in the chest, I lay the other out. Both hits ground -- out! I dra'em under the (railroad) car and ti'em good. But one'o'em was some cunt. Holy shit, I thought. I'm a lucky moth'a fucker today. I ripps her pants down with my knife. Marshall

In the above description, there was very little time to make a decision to rape his victim. In most of the serial rape accounts, it appears that the offenders are acting spontaneously. But serial rapists make decisions to commit the crime of rape hours, days, and/or possibly years prior to the actual attack. All that is lacking is opportunity. Therefore, predatory rape is a series of decisions leading to the actual assault for an offender. For instance, Marshall added:

> Damn, my hands starts mov'en everywhere. She starts yelling and yapping like a dog, so I slap's her good. She dud'it quit. She's really

nice! I pets her place (vagina). I put my thumbs over her eyes and tell her if she hurts me, I'll shoves them through her skull. I whip's out my man and feeds it to her. If she makes me come, I'll leave her be. That white trash knew her job. I was tot'en in a few minutes. We got the stuff from the (railroad) car and my partner goes down with her. I think he has (rapes) her and beats her. Marshall

Random victims included cases where a rapist found a victim while conducting other business including crimes such as robbery, criminal trespassing, and burglary. Due to the nature of random rape, lust appears to be the best predictor of serial rape under random conditions.

Situational Targeting

Situational targeting refers to victims found in a particular social environment or situation such as employment. In these cases, the offenders sought specific situations or circumstances as opposed to specific individuals to attack. The following remarks represent 9 accounts or 15% of the sample characterizing situational targeting.

I worked for this outfit that was to have a big meeting in DC and I was the guy who had to make the arrangements for it. I put a ad in one of the DC papers for models using a Pittsburgh modeling agency name, and the girls came to my free suite at the hotel on a certain day and time. Even the few times when the boards called the police, the hotels claimed they were hookers preying on poor convention managers, but the fact is they didn't want to lose my business. Howell

I travel a lot, ya know. Put a out-of-state tag on the front of my car and pull unto the driveway of houses that are being shown (For Sale). Once inside, if it's a babe show'en the place, I tell her that my wife and three kids are moving to the town. I might have to go to two or three house-openings to find the right woman. I leave. telling her I'm checking other houses out and come back just before she's ready to leave. Her defenses are down. Look the joint over again and grab her, tossing her to the floor. Usually I want her to suck me off cause I'm not going to screw something that can give me a disease. I don't like taking to much time by undressing her either. Sometimes I tie'em up and might jack off on her if I don't want her touch'en me. Horace

Situational rapists, like the other rapists in this sample, gave the impression that they had the intention of committing rape prior to finding their victims within a particular situation. For example:

When I was in college, I placed ads in different campus newspapers for models. If they refused sex and I really wanted them, I'd get'em high and take'em. I'd take pictures (Polaroid) in different positions. Later, if they'd say anything, I'd show'em the pictures. I liked the pictures sometimes more than sex with them. Sometimes I'd look at'em (the pictures) when I was hump'en one.

Sometimes, situational rapists use the occupation of a potential victim against her to get what they want—sex. For example, in the following description, the offender uses the victim's job by getting her to steal products from her employer and then intimidates her into sexual contact.

I watch'em in the stores like the mall. Especially the ones work'en the food places. Be nice to'em a few times when I buy shit. Smile. Say someth'en bout their looks. Watch'em. See if a boy friend comes. Ax'em to steel shit from work. Get'em involved. If she does it, no problem. I'll screw her and dump her. Ask? Ax her for sex instead of telling her she's going to do me? ...I'm already checking out other bitches and bringing them closer. I always got a few I'm work'en with.

In the following narration it might be easy to blame the victim. But, she is not the offender. What becomes clear is that due to her employment, she was more vulnerable to attack than other women. The following account also shows how situational rapists exploit females in a work environment.

They should have never released me from this psychiatric hospital for criminal cats like me. I played their game and I looked straight, but they never knew my secrets. Fools! When I got on the street, the first thing I did was find a place to sleep. It was a half-way house. The social workers they sent out from the university as trainees were slower than the idiots at the hospital. I told one I had pains behind my eyes and closed them tight. I fell on the floor and rolled around like I was having a fit. She held me and I turned her on her back and throw her dress up and ripped her panties in seconds. When I shot in her, I cried. I told I didn't know what happened. If she told, they'd send me back and I didn't want to go. I told her that the other prisoners raped me and that's why I lost control. She believed me and didn't report anything. Don't ask me how she looked, but she has sexy, sexy eyes that are hard to shake.

The descriptions above suggest that situational opportunities translate into predatory rape for the offenders and that their rapes are planned before locating a victim. Clearly, opportunity is vital to criminals. Criminals need victims available in order to attack, the intention of the attack is already present. Females who appear vulnerable are most likely to be attacked, and attack victims who learned helplessness are the victims most likely to be raped.

Confusing Statements

Sometimes, the descriptions of the predators were confusing, and I wasn't sure which victim selection category to put them in so I chose a "confusing" category. Below are two examples of a confusing victim selections.

When they say no, they don't mean it cause that's what they're best at. Gals love to screw probably more than men but they gotta be coy about it. Say'en no is a way they use to work a guy up that way they can say he owes. And I wanna tell ya about owing... buy a bitch a car, dinner, I don't care what and she says no after she get's the stuff so she can get more. They use their pussy like credit cards. Fred

When I was home alone or in a break-in, I'd go through dressers looking for women's clothes like shoes, girdles, bras, panties and stuff like that. I'd wear them or sometimes just stare at'em. I'd always smell'em. When I caught girls like fish'en with drugs at the play ground, I screw'em or make'em blow me when I wear'en my girlie things. I gave her drugs and brought my friends over before she knew what was happening. They all had her. But I never let my friends see my girlie stuff. Collin

In summary, if a sexual offender perceives a female to be vulnerable or if he can manipulate her into it, he will attack. Much of an offender's perception of vulnerability has to do with the nonverbal communication of the victim.

Target Conclusions

Blaming the victim for the behavior of a predator is not an acceptable answer under any condition. However, how an offender perceives his potential victim affects his decision to attack and how she responds during the attack will impact the outcome. Clearly, the information provided by the offenders suggests that they are constantly scanning their social landscapes and different opportunities in search of vulnerable females. They make many decisions, but all of those decisions impact the lives of other people. Predators fail more than they succeed in part because they spend more time thinking about the benefits of their attacks rather than planning them. Their attacks seem unplanned, crude, and spontaneous. They actually seem unmoved by their failures and keep trying to succeed. Clearly, serial rapists seek easy ways to get what they want—sex. The point is that females who present themselves as vulnerable and submit when attacked are at risk more than other females.

Predatory rapists reject violence as an attack technique because their crime would take longer, and they might get hurt. Most predatory rapists are wimps. Certainly, there are some predators who enjoy violence, but most predatory rapists are fearful parasites looking for helpless and willing victims.

Looking invincible and fighting back will change the outcome of most attacks. Government statistics shows that 3 out of 4 victims of rape successfully stop their attackers. Yet, I believe that each victim needs to make her own decision about resistance since it's easy to hand advice to others when you're not threatened. I not implying that victims who have submitted were foolish since life decisions are different than arm-chair decisions. However, what juries and law enforcement personnel need to know is that predatory rape is a conscious decision made by an individual who plays a numbers' game. The more females he intimidates, the more likely he wins—not because he's smart but because he's lazy, and because others believe that they are helpless against him, no matter what they do.

[1] Before going on, I should share that in an earlier study I included two categories not shown above: victim attractiveness and victim age. First this was an error. Second the error was that many of the statements which at first reflected victim attractiveness or victim age were perceived in relationship to one of the other categories. That is, less attractive women who were perceived as easy prey were more desirable than more attractive women who were not perceived as easy prey. Therefore, a victim's vulnerability, randomness, and/or situation were more important than looks, age, or her condition.

[2] This view is consistent with some of my earlier work suggesting that parents, especially middle class parents, tend to encourage their children to demand their rights as long as those rights do not interfere with the life-styles of their parents. See Stevens (1988). Also, see Frederick Elkin and Gerald Handel (1984).

[3] Also see Ira Schwartz (1989) who argues that parents at every socioeconomic level demand that law enforcement, school counselors, and social workers both guide and discipline their children for them.

CHAPTER SEVEN

VIOLENCE AND SERIAL RAPE

Overview of Violence

In the preceding chapter it was noted that much of the time how a serial rapist perceives potential victims affects his decision to attack. In this chapter it will be noted that how a victim responds during an attack, might affect the outcome of that attack. This chapter examines the extent of physical violence used by career rapists during their sexual attacks. While the offenders offered several descriptions of murder and necrophilla, overall, violence was selective and used sparingly by chronic rapists. An implication of this discovery is that "fear entrepreneurs" sensationalize the crime of serial rape.

Controversy continues about how much violence men use when they are sexually assaulting strangers. A review of the popular media as presented in an earlier chapter suggests that violence is the primary motive of predatory rape, and that therefore, females who are attacked should submit or face escalated violence. Is predatory sexual assault a fulfillment of violence or sexual appetites? One answer might come from government statistics that reveal that most predatory rape victims (both attempted and completed) are not physically injured during an assault. While most jurisdictions view rape as a crime of sexual misconduct sometimes involving passion, rape is also typically reported and examined as a crime of violence. Largely predatory rape may include descriptions about vaginal and anal penetration, cunnilingus, ejaculation, and fellatio, thus sexual offenders exhibiting those actions are classified as sexually dangerous. A number of individuals claim that predatory rape includes domination, force, and coercion indicating motivational factors such as violence and the need to gain control over a victim. Yet, some describe neurological disturbances as motivators or the arousal perspective. However, recent studies show that sexual fulfillment is largely responsible for sexual attacks upon vulnerable prey by unknown predators. Caution is stressed in these studies, because indicating that motives of career rapists can be far different than other classifications of rapists such as date rape, wife-rape, and the rape of children.

My assumptions are that predatory rapists are largely self-serving, demand instant gratification, care little about the needs of others, and as such exhibit little self-control; yet predatory rapists are in control of their facilities as they efficiently spend an enormous amount of time evaluating prey. But they are lazy and often care little about apprehended. Nonetheless, I believe that understanding offender violence can contribute to reduced victimization and improved offender rehabilitation.

Descriptions of Violence

When the descriptions of the offenders were examined together and the various levels of violence during their sexual attacks were measured, it appears that most of the respondents used violence sparingly when they assaulted their prey. Of course, there were numerous accounts that characterized various levels of violence. To better understand the role violence played in these attacks, I put the descriptions of the offenders into the following categories: unclear violence, nonviolence, intimidation, moderate, limited, and ultimate. Specifically, when the descriptions were placed into classifications characterizing violence (see Table 4), 18% (11) of the accounts were unclear. Thirteen percent (8) of the accounts characterized nonviolence; one criterion for this classification was that no where in these accounts was the use of force mentioned or implied before, during, and/or after the attack. Sixteen percent (10) of the rapists characterized intimidation as the only method used in their attacks, specifically threats used initially to shock victims into submission. Twenty percent (12) of these chronic offenders used physical contact or moderate violence, but only enough to get the attention of the victim. Another 20% (12) of the offenders said they used limited violence. These offenders used only enough force to obtain their victim's submission; once submission was granted, these offenders stopped using it. But these offenders, like all of the above, stopped their attacks when threatened. Finally, ultimate violence or aggravated force was reported in 13% (8) of the accounts before, during, and after the attacks. These individuals had no intention of stopping anything no matter what a victim did.

TABLE 4   TYPOLOGY OF VIOLENCE*   (N=61)

	PERCENTS	NUMBERS
Unclear	18%	11
Nonviolence	13%	8
Intimidation	16%	10
Moderate	20%	12
Limited	20%	12
Ultimate	13%	8
	100%	61

* The method used to arrange the categories of violence was guided by the descriptions of the offenders that characterized levels of violence as followed below.

Unclear Violence Levels

Also, in eighteen percent (11) of the accounts, it was unclear how much if any violence was utilized by the rapists. For example:

> It's a numbers game. Some... believe I'd hurt'em bad if they don't suck me. ...If they tell me to get fucked, I find another one and eventually find the one who believes me. I ain't ask'en no babe for sex, they go'en to do it and that's the end of that tune.

Nonviolence

Thirteen percent (8) of the accounts characterized nonviolent methods of gaining victim sexual submission by the rapists. These rapists said they had no physical contact other than the rape itself nor had they intimated their victims prior to their sexual success with them. For instance:

> We broke into this hospital drug store... I ducked into a room... Her body was hot... I saw in a movie where this guy... Before anything happens, the man (hospital guard) busts me for robbery, trespassing, and rape. I didn't screw the bitch. She told the judge that I messed with her, but no way, just felt her tits. Emory

> Each morn'en bout 9:00 to 12:00 when I'm on the move, I check motels out cause that's when the maids are clean'em up... I'd make people for small things. One time this honey was asleep, but I just looked till I decided to pull it (masturbated). She was asleep when I left, but I shot my wad on her. Stinger

These two examples are typical of all eight descriptions offered by nonviolent rapists.

Intimidation

Sixteen percent (10) of the offenders fall into a category of violence referred to as intimidation. That is, violence was not described by the offenders themselves before or after their sexual attack. Threats characterized as initially being used to shock victims into submission are represented by the following account.

> I follow some cute babe from the parking lot at a mall. Inside, I walk up to her and ask if she owns such an' such car with such an' such tag. Maybe I describe someth'en' on the seats. I ask her bout the small animal locked in... We almost run to it... I'll say, you know what happens next. You can get hurt or it'll be over soon. She goes down on me [oral sex], and I disappear after I... Tyrone

Many of these offenders used intimidation, but only used it to shock their victims into sexual submission. Their main goal appears to be sexual intimacy with their victims.

Moderate Violence

Twenty percent (12) of the offenders characterize physical contact but only enough to get the attention of the victim. A typical statement made by the offenders who fit this category follows:

> I called for appointments at doctor and dentists offices in another town. Their nurses would tell me when they had openings... I went to the offices when I knew the docs weren't in and three times I found a nurse'y alone. I'd made up a story about pain in my mouth, one time, and when she looked, I grabbed her hands and throw her on the floor. You know what happens next, I said to her. I had intercourse with her in the dentist's chair. Told her if she opens her mouth I'd be back, get it... opens her mouth! (He laughed. Note: he was never apprehended for these crimes).

It appears that most of the criminals who typified moderate violence rejected violence themselves and would, if confronted, stop their attack. Sexual

74

contact was clearly their goal. Also, sometimes the inmates explain how the threat
of a weapon would also be utilized to gain submission.

> If she's not watching what's happening all around her, then doesn't
> know how to handle herself, how to use the things around her to
> hurt me or get me caught. Sometimes I can go to them on the street
> and say shit like, okay, bitch... you know what I want and if you
> don't give it to me, I've got a gun in my pocket that says you're
> dead. I'll get in their car or they'll get in mine. If I do white stuff,
> she won't tell. O'Henry

Moderate offenders use a blow, a push, a slap, or threaten the use of a
weapon to reach their objectives. Some of the offenders describe no physical
contact with their victims other than sexual contact. Serial rapists used only
enough physical contact to get the attention of the victims, but others used
intimidation to obtain their goals.

Limited Violence

Twenty percent (12) of the offenders can be characterized as limited
violent type rapists. One criterion for this category is that physical abuse was used
more than necessary to gain victim submission but the abuse could stop when the
attacker was threatened. Also, these offenders used violence to shock a victim into
submission. For instance, Jake explains:

> I saw this fine lookin broad in the parking lot carrying a load of
> food with a little kid hanging on... I pushed her into the car and
> grabbed the kid by the throat. I slid in on top of her and said to the
> bitch, if you ain't a good little girl, I'll kill the kid. She said
> something to me that I didn't understand, so I slammed the shit out
> of her first with my free hand. Jake

Jake is using more force than necessary to push his victim into sexual submission. However, he, like the other rapists who describe limited violence, can hardly take refuse in his violence as he explains further: "I told her, I want you to suck my cock. She started to but the kid won't shut up so I cracked it and she started crying too. I ran." The use of violence and submission and/or the use of a weapon both serve as a guide to put certain serial rape accounts into this category. For example:

> If they submit when I go for it, fine. When they refuse, I put a gun to their forehead. If they still say no, I smack'em with my gun. They always say yes. One time, this sweety goes no, so I said fuck you and left.

Limited violence suggests that there is a limit to the amount of violence these men would use to meet their objective. Their attack can be stopped unlike the individuals described in the ultimate violence category. Other offenders, too, show that violence was used sparingly to get their way as in the cases of moderate violence accounts.

Ultimate Violence

Thirteen percent (8) of the 61 heinous offenders described their forcible rape attacks with an emphasis on acts of violence before, during, and after their assaults. These offenders showed they lacked limits or control in their attacks. However, these offenders were in control of themselves and in touch with reality—a reality developed and executed in a systematic process to destroy another human being in a variety of ways. In fact, in the descriptions of these violators, the destruction of human dignity and/or a human being was the dual goal of the offender, and sexual acts feed from the activities. For example:

> She was carrying a lot of packages... I open my van. ...my gun's look'en at her tits. From my rape case, I take out handcuffs... I took

a cord from my case and tied her ankles pulling it up to her wrests.
I had to check in at home so I let her in the van. Barney

One tool characteristic by these offenders is anger or ultimate hatred for women. This rage continues long past victim subjugation and in some cases—long past the death of their victims. Rage blinds their violence and acts as an alibi to exercise their destruction of another human being. Why did Barney wait to complete the act? Maybe part of his systematic technique to destroy another human being is to hold his victim hostage thus breaking down her resistance and her dignity. Continuing his narration, Barney's mission materializes further in his account.

> In the middle of the night I left my warm bed and had anal sex with her (in the van). Her shit was on my stick (penis) so I made her lick it off. I choked her until she past out, and did it several more times. In the morning I had to take my daughters to school so I used my wife's car. When I got back, I went for a ride (in the van). Out at the city dump, I had intercourse with her and choked her again till she past out. ...I shaved her pussy clean and shoved my new hamper inside her. I got the handle into her rectum and moved it around a lot like a joy stick. Barney

Obviously sexual contact is not a significant event of the abduction, he has prioritized the systematic punishment he inflicts on his victim. He demonstrated little regard for his victim as a human being as he follows through with a seemingly proven plan of destruction. Like other violent abusers, he ignores the humanity of his victims. His victim is the recipient whose function is to absorb his rage and anger. Barney, like others in this category, commit the crime of rape in an effort to deal with unresolved and conflicted aspects of life. Also, rape can be an expression of power and an assertion of strength and manhood. Do criminals play a role (they created) or read from a script (they wrote) when committing criminally violent behavior? Fenney's account lends some help in understanding this question:

I tried fuck'en this cat when I was little but the fuck'en thing scratched the fuck. out'a me. I grabbed that moth'a fuck'ag and popped its fucken eyes out. I stuck my dick in its asswhole. Shit, when I shoot it was like... burning fuck'en lights in my head. Damn... I still se'em but I ain't going to put my dick in anything without eyes... Everyday man, there's this shit in my head. Legs, asses, and foreheads of things – fuck'en things that ain't mov'en no more. Fenney.

He reversed his role with animals and played it out with dead victims. Several times, when he was younger, he had brought road-kill home. He caked it (maggots and all) around his penis, and masturbated into the mass. Other times, he, like some of the other sadistic rapists discussed in Chapter Eight, used animals to conduct sexual experiments on. Sometimes they killed the animals before their experiments and other times they killed them during their experiences. To say the least, their ideas about reality seem to be highly distorted. Necrophilla was once thought to be rare, but it is being seen more and more in the accounts of serious offenders. My guess is that many of the serial rapists in this category also committed the act of necrophilla, but only 2 of the participants actually described necrophilla activities with human beings. It is safe to say that Fenney, and rapists like him, used a great deal of fantasy before, during, and after his encounter with his victims.

CONCLUSION

Of the 61 cases showing various methods used by the offenders to gain victim submission, over one-half used violence sparingly for the purpose of shocking victims into sexual submission. Violence or weapons served a fundamental purpose to promote the main objective—sex.

The sensationalized accounts of violent rape incite the public with misconceptions of serial rape. Maybe these fear entrepreneurs have hidden agendas that don't include the well being of the victim. Nonetheless, based on the accounts of the respondents in this study, the lesson is to fight and never submit.

What also emerged from the data in this study is the fact that predators spend most of their lives in pursuit of their perversions which does not necessarily include violence. Career criminals live one life—the life of a criminal every minute or every day. All events of their lives relate to crime. Yet, most of the respondents in this study were never apprehended for their sexual attacks and at this writing, most of them have been released from the penitentiary.

CHAPTER EIGHT

EXCESSIVE FORCE

Assumptions of Human Behavior

My assumptions are that predatory rapists are self-serving, care little about apprehension, and less about the needs of others. They exhibit little self-control during the attack. But, the range of self-regulated behavior which they exhibit depends on the boundaries they have placed on themselves and the goals they're after. If they see violence as inappropriate, they might use intimation and/or manipulation to assault, torture, and sometimes murder. Sometimes their interest is with necrophilla and other times with cannibalism. This chapter will examine those offenders who have placed no limits on their actions. Like other predatory offenders, they are in control of their facilities to the extent that they efficiently spend enormous amounts of time seeking an opportunity to commit crime. Most serial rapists operate in a similar style but with self-directed limits. Each rapist, regardless of his style, continually scans his social environment for an opportunity to attack vulnerable prey.

Some experts suggest that human behavior is a result of initiating factors such as attitudes, need-dispositions, and/or unconscious complexes.[1] One explanation about human behavior is that it results from a process of interactions or exchanges by which we experience our world. We create our own social reality in response to our understanding of what we see, hear, and/or feel. We respond based on those understandings or interpretations, directed by our goals, limited by our physical capabilities, personal experiences, and level of expertise.[2] To better understand the rapist who uses excessive force, their accounts hold answers.

Excessive Force Offenders

Most of the offenders in each category described behavior that characterized intimation or the use of violence sparingly, if at all, during attacks. When their victims threatened or fought back, most of the offenders stopped their attacks as quickly as they began them. But, 13% (8) of the offenders described supremacy rape and ultimate violence (both were discussed in the previous chapter). These offenders aggravated the use of force before, during, and after victim submission. The intention of these offenders was never to stop their attack—no matter how a victim responded or the condition their victim was in including her own death. These offenders lack limits or controls in their destruction of others, and since they eroticized their criminally violent behavior, I will refer to these offenders as sadistic rapists. However, these descriptions demonstrate that the offender is in control of himself and in touch with reality—a reality while entirely inappropriate is developed and executed in a systematic process to destroy another human being in a variety of ways. The destruction of human dignity and/or a human being is the dual goal of the sadistic offender, and sexual acts feed from the activities leading to their goals (also see Chapters 5 & 7 for other descriptions of excessive violence). For example:

> Home sweet home, mom and her kid were walking down... My gun pointed at the kid... On a deserted road out of town, I stopped and told her I'd fuck her son in the ass if she didn't have sex with me. When I was pumping away like the beautiful man I am, I told her to suck her kid. No...,, I slapped the whore. You owe me, bitch... Suck his dick or you're go'en watch that child die. Man... that got me off watch'en her do tat. When her kid came, I beat the fuck out'a both of'em and took them back to the street where I got'em from. Told that whore, you ever call the po'lice, I be back and I will fuck your kid in the ass. Then, I'll fuck your husband too. Jesse (Note: was never charged with this crime).

One characteristic of these offenders was anger or an ultimate hatred for women. This rage continues long past victim subjugation and in some cases—

long past the death of their victims. Rage blinds them and operates, as does the actual sexual assault, to exercise their destruction of another human being.

If these chronic offenders wanted only sexual contact from their victims, why do they wait to complete the act? Part of the systematic technique to destroy another human being is to hold the victim hostage thus breaking down resistance and dignity. For instance:

> See I have a few drinks and go limp likes a noodle. I like to beat'em with belts and burn'em with cigarettes. Fact is, when cunts obey... I get harder. This cunt I met at a bar was in for a surprise when I took her to a party and gave her a (an) enema in front (of) my friends. I know she loved it but she screamed like a child. Most of them had (raped) her later. I got her really high on good shit and kicked her ass out of my car in the worst part of town. I came around the corner and pretended I didn't know her. My partner pulled her fuck'en head through the (side) window of my car. My partner held her head as I fucked her from the street with my fist. We drove off. He told me that he jerked off when he hold her head and came on her face. Far as I know, she's still there. George (Note: he implied that he was never charged with this crime).

George inflicted systematic punishment on his victim. He demonstrated little regard for his victim as a human being. He was able to rise above humanity—especially the humanity of his victims. These offenders attacked prey in order to deal with personal, unresolved and conflicted aspects of their lives. Also, the attack was an expression of power and an assertion of strength and manhood as evidenced by George's descriptions.

Violence is, indeed, a quicker and a shorter way for many of the rapists in this study to get what they want, but especially for the sadistic rapist. These violent criminals gained neither power nor sexual intimacy, although they exerted power and sex. Power through sexual contact links to the ultimate goal of destruction of other human beings in a variety of ways. For example, the destruction of other human beings through violence is, in essence, the objective of these predators as characterized by the following account:

It was weird. I couldn't stop. Kind'a like in dreams. I wasn't pounding (raping) the bitch. It was like somebody else. Eddy came back (from the front seat of the car) and put it to her, too. They thought I killed her because they never heard her scream. Kicked the bitch out at (an) interstate turnoff and made sure no one saw us. But damn, some fregg'en trooper pulled us over for a tail light being out and saw the bitch's purse and blood all over me. Albert

Yet, the descriptions of the participants seem to suggest that they followed a script or played a role. For example:

We went to my room in a motel... Two girls and a guy; the guy was married to one of the bitches. They had some good dope... we was like real high, but I knew the rest of story. I grabbed one...stop, she yelled again... Her eyes just burned into me, and she tried to slide away. I slapped her hard a lot of times and went for her throat. I squeezed it... She goes, why me. Fuck you, I says...Tears flooded... Her girl friend looks over while she get'en screwed and goes someth'en like, give in... I squeezed the little whore till the slut past out. Once my cock jammed this piece of trash, I let go of the neck. When the guy slept, I crawled over (to the other bed) and spread the other one (girl) out. She said someth'en like, don't. ...smacked her (too). I shoved it in. The guy (girl's husband) like wakes. He was like dazed. I punched the fucker - hard. He didn't move. So I came (ejaculated) on his face. Pushed his slut queen's fuck'en head in it and told her to lick it. I am the 'man' in their lives they'll never forget. I'm a bad moth'a'f...'a, bad! Before I go, I pulled the fuck'en nipple of the other bitch and jammed the (writing) pen through it. Took their fuck'en drugs and money and split. Nick

Nick was playing a role—the role of a very bad man. He demonstrated to each of his victims that he was in control and the most significant person in their lives ("I am the man in their lives they'll never forget"). He was playing a god-like role typical of the other rapists who knew few restraints. Do sadistic rapists play a god-like role when committing corrupt acts? Ted's account lends some further help in understanding this question:

I got started messing women's bodies up when I was young. I'd cut pictures of women, along their body lines, from the Sears catalog. Then I'd cut body parts from Playboy or one of those. When I wanted to undress the pure women in Sears. I'd use the nude parts from Playboy or Hustler so I could see her face but her body was naked. Sometimes I'd cut men's dicks out and add'em to the pictures. I'd see the face of the pure women, the body from Playboy and a man's dick sticking out from her. I could take other women, undress her and play with the cut-outs so that it would look like a woman with a man's thing, screw'en another woman. When I was older, I'd make appointments with women lawyers and shrinks. If they looked like any of the women I created, I'd think about it when I made myself come. A couple of times, I played real stupid and non-threatening. I made my move and pulled out my gun forcing this pure lawyer bitch to the floor. Shit, just telling you about it is getting me up (erect)! I dressed an undressed her in her office. Ted

Ted created a social reality that related to his past experiences. In the rest of his narrative, he fulfilled his role objectives. For instance:

I pulled out some of my pictures that were taped together and laid them on her face. I masturbated and came on her being careful not to hit my pictures. She wasn't so pure when I got done with her. I never got caught because I kept moving around. One time though I cut her up and wanted to put her body parts onto another women, but I had to stop because I really didn't want to hurt her. I hated myself for being a coward so I shot her and moved to another town...

We see that Ted has created an illusion about his expectations of both his real victim and his imagined victim. These accounts offer compelling testimony of what "a bad moth'a'fuc'a" is to these offenders. Clearly their idea is culturally defined and individually initiated. These offenders think that they are playing a role of sorts during their attacks. Perhaps by knowing the outcomes of their behavior, we can see that these offenders are acting from a script they wrote. For example, Ted revealed:

> Yea, sure... I screwed her good. Her blood was all over me, the pig, so I slapped her... know what? She couldn't hit me back! ...maybe, there were others like her. ...I told yea, doc, yea. I had sex with her when she was dead not because I'm weird, but because I could make her face look like my pictures. I set her face up with a smile or whatever and that's the way she'd look. ...I'd cut eyes of my girls and put them over her closed eyes that way she watched me and smiled the whole time. Got it? Ted

When Ted performed the role of an "attacker," he perceived the appropriate behavior for that role or what can be called a self-fulfilling prophecy. He acted out the obligations and expectations of an attacker and/or the obligations of "a bad moth'a'fuc'a." When his victim did not meet the perceived obligations and expectations of her role as the victim, he interjected his own expectations on her.

Although only two of the participants actually described necrophilla activities, I suspect that the ultimate violence rapists also committed these acts. However, necrophilla is a description not a causal factor to these violent acts. Clearly, finding satisfaction by degrading, beating, and sometimes killing a victim, then engaging in sexual contact with that victim (human or animal, see Finney's account in Chapter 7) takes patience, skill, and motivation. Above all, it takes playing a role of an offender who has eroticized these activities. In that way, the offender rises above humanity and sees himself as something more than a human being. "Me," revealed Smitty, "bit'en a piece of meat off'a dead cunt, I've just blew my wad (ejaculation) in, shows that I'm good and bad—the worst nightmare she's ever come across." The accounts of these rapists were consistent with Ted Bundy and Edward Gein in that both offenders thought they were inherently evil in themselves.[3] Thus, the role they're playing may not be god-like but devil-like.

An Evil Role

Criminally violent offenders, who use excessive force, often commit the crimes of murder, rape, and necrophilla with the same victim. They create their own illusion of reality; often times the meaning, relevance, and goals of these illusions are only known by an individual offender. These illusions are usually guided by the experiences of an offender through a process of trial and error and personal assessment—an assessment or interpretation of the world furthered by role expectations and obligations. To learn the extent of an offender's criminal history might be to discover his attitudes about the expectations and obligations of the role he plays especially when attacking others. If he thinks he is a god or the devil then it might lead to the life or death of others are both of which are within his perceived province.

Simply explaining supremacy or control and power via violence, the popular view as found in magazines, newspapers, and Hollywood as a causal model, leaves many questions. Good social science research should show what is obvious, rather than offering popular explanations.[4] For example, an individual who destroys other human beings sees himself as an individual above the law of both man and God. He sees himself as playing the role of evil, it could be argued from the descriptions of the offenders. Therefore, to re-examine a naturalistic analysis in terms of supernatural dimensions might provide one answer. This is not an invitation to examine demonic or supernatural beliefs of ancient civilizations. But it is an invitation to think beyond the confines of a purely naturalistic view that often becomes preoccupied with testable explanations of things in this world and forgets to consider their moral, spiritual, or cosmic dimensions. The role of evil or demonic possession with all its inhuman characteristics could be believable when trying to understand how criminals can easily surpass the very nature of being human by performing some of the activities as those revealed in this study. But there is a major deficit in criminal research or investigation by which to judge the evils of the modern criminal.[5] Many sophisticated theories are probably in the dark about violence, partly due to the conservative nature of some writers and the difficulty of publishing other than traditional ideas. A few writers have examined the role of evil as an explanation for various crimes.[6] Yet, few writers specifically write about evil and serial rape. In fact, there appears to be a "sacred void" in both the research and in the crime lab about evil and fulfilling the role of evil. Stanford Lyman continues this thought:

> Evil is a term that is rarely found in a modern sociology text... To the extent that sociological thought embraces the study of evil today, it does so under the embarrassing, neutered morality of deviance. Adopting for the most part an uncritical stance toward the normative structure of any given society, the... sociologist of deviance takes his cue from whatever the forces of law and restriction define as evil. Hence, the concerns of the vocal and powerful elements of a society become the resources for a sociological investigation of evil (1989. p.1).

Serial rapists who engage in criminally violent behavior such as sadistic rapists are men moved by a force that I will refer to as evil. My definition of evil includes a range of behavior from attacking human dignity to destroying human life. Whether the evil the participants possess originated outside of them or is created by them is insignificant to the results of their behavior. More than likely, these individuals have produced their own sense of corruption in that they have taken the role of the devil. My subjects perceived themselves as evil and acted accordingly. As suggested by W. I. Thomas, if individuals "define situations as real, they are real in their consequences."

By showing how violent and corrupt they can be, the more they perceived they are evil. Doing corrupt acts makes them unique and special. Therefore, ugly sadistic rape is their way "of making a mark upon God's world." It's their way of telling others that they are significant in this world. In a sense, acting evil can be the opposite of acting divine. For example, necrophilla involves holding a god-like power (the opposite of evil) over an individual.

Charles Manson, Ted Bundy, and Pee Wee Gaskins have told us much about their relationship with evil. In Pee Wee's terms, "I am god - the god of death." He and others believe it. They have told themselves and have demonstrated to themselves and others how bad and corrupt they are. Many violent offenders tend to describe themselves as "I'm bad, mannn, real bad!" These men have accepted an evil role, and will do everything to prove it.[7]

Can ordinary people become extraordinarily evil in their behavior? Some of my recent research suggests that nonviolent offenders can become violent offenders as a result of being incarcerated. Fred Katz suggests that non-criminals or ordinary people can engage in evil too. He claims that only a tiny proportion of this century's massive killings are attributable to the actions of people we call criminals, crazy people, or socially alienated, or even people we identify as evil people. The vast majority of killings were actually carried out by plain folks in the population, ordinary people like you and me. Certainly the Hitlers and Stalins of our world produced plans for evil, but who transformed those plans into action? Hitler and his followers donated their energies, their skill, and their very lives to carry out the evil.

Two points can be made about sadistic rapists who utilize excessive force and commit murder during a serial rape attack: (1) rehabilitation is futile; and (2) only their total destruction will stop them. However, it should be noted that most serial rapists use force sparingly if at all. Further research is called for on the detection of serial rapists.

Many violent offenders demonstrate criminally violent characteristics when they are four or five years old, according to Stanton Samenow.[8] It would seem logical therefore to spend our enormous law and order expenditures on our children rather than on our offenders. Government statistics report that the United States spends far more money on police and corrections than on teachers, schools, and family well being. Certainly, if American society redirects its resources to its young, then adults will not need to purchase weapons or if they do they can receive the necessary training to use those weapons effectively.

[1] Brownmiller, 1975; Burgess & Holmstrom, 1974; Ellis, 1989; Groth, 1979; Groth & Burgess, 1980; Storaska, 1975.

[2] For a closer look see Herbert Blumer's (1969) notion of Symbolic Interactionism which suggests that human behavior is a product of an individual's interpretation of his or her social environment. Human behavior can consist of meeting a flow of situations in which individuals have to act, and that their behavior is built on the basis of what they note, assess, interpret, and what kind of projected lines of behavior they map out for themselves.

[3] See Ann Rule (1980) for accounts on Ted Bundy, Judge Robert H. Gollmar (1981) for accounts on Edward Gein, and Gaskins, (1994) for accounts on Pee Wee Gaskins. For FBI accounts of celebrated cases see Douglas and Olshaker (1995).

[4] For a closer reading on this thought see writers like Peter L. Berger (1963). Then, too, has not history taught us that the ideas of some individuals like those of Socrates, Jesus, Mohammed, Galileo, Marx, and Dr. Martin Luther King, Jr. were considered radical and insane by others in their day. The question remains: why would certain individuals in our society utilize so much systematic force to destroy another human being?

[5] For more information on this perspective see Stanford Lyman (1978).

[6] Recently, some writers exam evil as explanations for various crimes, yet none talk specifically about the relationship between serial rape and evil (Heller, Stamatiou, & Puntscher-Riekmann, 1993; Katz, 1993; Katz, 1988; Giacoia, 1992; Zukier, 1994).

[7] See Ann Rule (1980) for accounts on Ted Bundy, see Judge Robert H. Gollmar (1981) for accounts on Edward Gein, and see Gaskins (1994) for accounts on Pee Wee Gaskins.

[8] Samenow (1984) discusses Anti Social Personality Disorder in a clear and precise manner without using the technical terms. His work explains that many of the disorder's characteristics are salient at age 5 and that appropriate parental guidance can help future outcomes of that child. One question I might have about his work is that his sample group was incarcerated and it is likely that many participants in his study learned the characteristics of ASPD while confined. I have used this book as required reading for all of my criminal majors for the past 10 years.

CHAPTER NINE

INSIDE THE HEAD OF A RAPIST

To better understand the strategies embraced by chronic sexual offenders, their typical lifestyle experiences require attention. What follows is a typical life profile of a sexual offender as he experienced youth, manhood, and prison. This composite provides a window into the compelling dynamics that shape the faulty decision making processes of a sexual offender. His name is Darin, and he will be out of prison by the time you read these pages. He served four years and two months for assault and theft as well as all of the crimes against women and children. Darin is a slight man, weighing one hundred and thirty pounds, close to five feet nine inches tall. He smiles endlessly about anything including the plague. When he is still, people might guess his age at 32, but when he talks he seems younger. He is an intense listener with a steady smile and piercing round eyes that lock on yours almost as if he were a priest. When he talks, his voice chimes with a freshness that gives the impression he is a bright college graduate starting his first job, even when he's describing his crimes. Descriptions such as handsome, charming, and sensitive are used by police officers who arrested him, correctional officers who guard him, and psychologists who evaluated him. His victims called him manipulative and dangerous. He is a predator who can never be cured.

His parents met at high school, graduated a year apart from each other, married before they were twenty, and now live several blocks from their early childhood homes. Darin has a younger brother and sister. His parents were often away from home, his aging grandmother and aunt watched over them. Nonetheless, Darin, a very active child, was alone most of the time since his grandmother and aunt favored his passive brother and sister. When his parents were home, they quarreled bitterly and threw things at each other. Darin often found refuge in a cluttered closet. His brother and sister found haven with their aunt.

Before first grade Darin experienced masturbation; it brought him immediate relief and feelings of serenity. A lack of attention gave him the opportunities to explore his sexuality, fantasies, and feelings. As Darin grew, he looked inward for comfort, withdrawing from others and outside activities. The outside world was a bitter disappointment prolonging his stress and hardships. The more he withdrew, the more he felt alienation and frustration and the more he lied about his behavior, his whereabouts, and his desires.

At school, since academics came easy to him, he focused on observing others while most students focused on teachers, workbooks, and rules. For instance, Darin studied the teacher and students while everyone else followed a reader in their literature book. He also learned by "doing and taking chances." Once he put on the coat of another student to wear it home. He was caught before leaving school. He often said shocking things to students to watch their reactions. Another way he learned about behavior was by playing the class clown; being funny allowed him access to every personality in the class. When other boys challenged him to a fight, Darin was able to make them his allies with the rational of a combat commander. Fighting was not one of Darin's strengths.

At home when he masturbated, he tried to recall the response of a girl at school to his earlier antics. This was his way of being intimate with a girl without having to deal with her. At school the next day, he stared at the girl while trying to recall his ejaculation, but he never could. He wanted to be satisfied without exhausting much effort.

When Darin was in sixth grade, he often babysat Tammy, a 4 year old girl who lived next door, while her mother went on errands. Tammy's father lived elsewhere. He wondered how much Tammy would like to bite his penis and how large her eyes would grow when he "shot" (ejaculated) in her month. Each time he babysat, he got braver. He decided that she liked being touched everywhere especially her back. He smoothed his index finger on the outside of her vagina and tried to push his fingers in her. He stopped because he saw droplets of blood coming from her little body. He studied each careening droplet with intensity, he recalled. He tried to convince me that he felt sorry for the pain Tammy experienced. Several times he ejaculated on her bare buttock as he pretended to spank her. A few times he ejaculated on her face. He recalled one time wiping her face quickly as he heard her mother's vehicle enter their garage. He tickled Tammy forcing a wide smile as her mother walked into the kitchen. Tammy's mother kissed her cheek, the very cheek he had wiped semen from. When asked how he felt about that experience, a huge smile crowded his face. He continued to discuss the experience with the urgency of a used car salesman. Darin said that he wondered how Tammy and her mother would look having sex together. Years later, when Darin attacked a woman and her young son, he remembered the "cheek experience." He said that he became so excited by its memory that he frightened the woman into oral sex with her son. Darin raped her and maculated the boy.

Darin often engaged in house break-ins, shoplifting, and school vandalism alone. He liked the idea that he could outsmart adults by committing crimes, although he never referred to them as crimes. just games. Every so often he tried different drugs including uppers and downers but didn't like the effect they had on him. To outwit others and to avoid apprehension, he had to be in control of himself. However, he often lost control of himself when he had intercourse and most of the time, it was "my duty to come deep inside her body," Darin proclaimed. Forced intercourse was his obsession and salvation. Even when he might masturbate, he rammed his penis in the vagina of his victim when he ejaculated, "to get her fluids on me. That made me harder in the days ahead." Weeks after a forced sexual encounter with a female, he had little difficulty getting an erection. But several weeks after the attack, becoming erect could happen only if he attacked another female. Prison was an excellent laboratory!

Darin was not able to have forced sex with females, and consequently was rarely erect although he did have sexual relations with other inmates. He described experiences that seemed to relate to a drug addict instead of a sexual offender. Might there be a correlation between forced intercourse and addiction?

When he was in ninth grade, he and Tammy played many games together such as baker and doctor. He waited for an opportunity to teach her how to make him have an ejaculation using her hands. He tried many ways during the games and finally succeeded. He convinced Tammy that she was a bad girl, and he would tell her mother. As expected, she cried and cried until he promised he wouldn't tell. "Let's keep it our secret," he said. Molesting the child was a simple task after that—no more games. Next, he taught her how to make him have an ejaculation using her mouth, but he usually had to masturbate and feed his penis into her mouth.

At 16, he pretended to be asleep on Tammy's mother couch when he heard her arrive at home after a date. She was in the washroom on the toilet when he attacked her. He was unsuccessful. He cried, telling her that he thought of her as his mother and that he didn't know why he behaved the way he had. She forgave him. Weeks later, he broke into her home, filled the bathtub with water, waited for her to come home from work, and emerged himself in the water pretending to commit suicide. She saved him. He could still talk about the kindness of her touch. Occasionally when he thought about her rescue, he pricked his scrotum with a sewing pin when he masturbated.

Several months later, he crawled through a window and attacked her as she slept. The police were called. Darin cried and wailed in pain. He said that the woman often forced him into having oral sex and that this time he refused. After an investigation, they charged her with felony rape. Darin refused to testify, and the charges against her were dropped.

He eventually moved from his childhood home, but returned to rape his neighbor two more times. The third time, as she slept he tied a noose around her neck. He dragged her from bed to the floor, and choked her until she performed oral sex while Tammy watched until he locked her in the closet. He tied Tammy's mother to the bed, shoved some amphetamines down her throat, pushed a few straight-pins thorough her nipples, and sexually assaulted her with sex toys. He said he wanted to show her that he was an adult and not a child. He also said that he was angry that she had betrayed him by calling the police on him in the past. Now he wanted to call the police and this time, "I will testify," he sniveled repeatedly in her ear. As his last act, he brought Tammy back into the bedroom and pulled her pajamas from her. He put the large sex toy close to her vagina, "If you report me, I'll be back," he said. He stole several items from her home and threw them in the river on his way to his uptown apartment.

As a student at a local community college, Darin took an internship at a summer children's camp. He sexually attacked a boy and a girl. He succeeded with the boy but could not have an ejaculation although he was erect. Darin told his victim that he must be a homosexual and had brought the attack upon himself by attacking Darin with "a secret fag eye beam." Darin said that he wouldn't tell the others about the incident if the boy didn't use his beam on others and if he remained in his room pretending to be sick. Darin visited him several times, but did not have sex with him. He tightly held the boy and stroked his hair, even though he believed that the boy enjoyed their earlier sexual encounter.

Largely, Darin maintained temporary friendships and avoided females who lacked an aggressive nature. He exaggerated friendships and relationships with aggressive girls in order to manipulate them to be his sexual partner. What he liked about aggressive girls was that they were strong willed and could manipulate his penis as forcefully as he had, but some of those females wanted to be satisfied too. He wasn't interested in mutual satisfaction. Since he didn't want or know how to behave in an ongoing relationship nor did he want to, most of those relationships ended soon after they began. To Darin people who understood him were threats, but acquaintances were impressed with his charm. He hated being charming. Several times Darin tried to kill himself but he never succeeded. Since he laughed while he explained each of those occurrences, I took that to mean that he could have used those events to manipulate others.

Darin had a brief sexual affair with one of his male instructors at the community college. Darin was easily lured into the relationship but soon dominated it. He took the instructor's credit cards and used his car for a month. Darin told the man that he would tell everyone about their relationship if he reported him. Darin also had sexual relations with other homosexuals he had met through his teacher. Shortly thereafter, the instructor quit his job and moved to away, or so Darin maintained. When the instructor's mother and others inquired as to his whereabouts, he lied and kept the secret affair from everyone including the police when they investigated the disappearance of the college instructor.

Sex in itself was boring, but rape got him what he wanted—forced sexual intercourse. He believed that he had given his victims what they wanted, too. In answer to the question about committing predatory rape, he said: "It's difficult to describe something invisible stirring inside your belly reaching into the muscle-lining of your throat demanding I do something! Deciding, all right tonight, I'll cruise and find some morsel to feed you. Leave me be. Festival (his term for sexual attacks) is near."

Attacking a female was the only way of feeling good and eventually he decided that his female victims felt good about his attack as well since they submitted easily to his demands. In his mid-twenties he performed well at work, but he could never get sexual attacks out of his head.

He married a woman he met at work. She worked in the mailroom. He was a rising executive. People often asked Darin why he married a woman older and heavier than himself. He told them that "love is greater than fat!" The first time they dated, she got drunk and he raped her. Their sexual relationships were usually on a roller coaster depending on how Darin felt. He practiced some of his attack holds on her to see which ones worked and which ones didn't.

Every so often, he drove or flew to different destinations to attack females. Sometimes he attacked vulnerable females and sometimes he tried to manipulate others into vulnerable situations, but mostly he failed. Most of his victims worked in offices in small strip malls and a few in motels and restaurants. He succeeded every few months and was almost apprehended once. The way he described his feelings was:

> Everything that flows through my mind, every image swallowed by my brain, every smell. is focused on festival. I must smell the fright of a woman when she knows she's going to give in because that's what god made her for—and I must taste her sweat when I finish her off because she worked so hard to please me. They love it doc; they really love being forced. But, I'm dying a thousand deaths in here (prison) because I need… a girl, any girl to love.

The last time Darin held his young daughter during a prison visit, he wondered how much she wanted to put her lips around his penis and how large her eyes would get when he would shoot inside her mouth. He loved her smell and couldn't get her scent out of his mind for several months.

CHAPTER TEN

CONCLUSION

Popular writers suggest control, power, and violence are the primary objectives of predatory rapists. They advocate that women should never resist predators; that a victim can expect escalated violence and sometimes death should they resist. These ideas are largely unsupported by serial rapists.

One reason for this serious difference of opinion is that fear entrepreneurs sensationalize predatory rape and others "politicize" it. In fact, government statistics reveal that most serial rape victims are never injured during a predatory rape. Possibly, popular writers and their politically correct partners created an information rape cartel centered in a group think process which they can not reject for fear of looking ill advised. They are the writers who suggest that all men are potential rapists! After the average god-fearing male reads the accounts of predators in this study and thinks he's anything like the men in this study, then it might be safe to say that all women are potential whores, and we know that isn't true either!

Is human conduct, such as the conduct of a serial rapist, a result of an initiating set of diabolical factors such as majestic cultural objectives, mysterious unconscious complexes energized by DNA deposits, and/or subliminal stimuli configurations? Frankly, one practical way to understand behavior is that it largely results from a continual process of self-interaction through individual interpretation of an environment. Each of us decide on a response that best brings us closer to our goal (for the moment), and do it—limited by our physical capabilities, personal experiences, and level of expertise. Behavior changes depending on how we see or interpret a situation linked to our goals. Yet humans are oriented towards a goal.[1] Therefore, in order to commit a crime, it takes intent first and opportunity second, not the other way around.

Serial rape should never be viewed as an isolated event should we wish to control predators. Predatory rape is a series of ongoing conscious decisions made by a predator. A forced sexual encounter with a female is the goal of the predator fueled by a psychological dependence and possibly, a physiological dependence. A vulnerable appearing female will set off an unavoidable attack. Power, control, and violence are merely interpretations of popular writers' explanations about most serial rapists. Most attacks can be stopped when the victim doesn't think or act like a victim.

Most predatory rapists I interviewed understood their feelings, their experiences, and the consequences of their criminal behavior. Simply put, like most human conduct, rapists said that there were no giant mysteries surrounding their sexual attacks. Tragically, most of them would have stopped what they were doing if they chose or if their victims fought back. For one, if a female fought her attacker she would feel better regardless of the outcome of the attack.[2] For a very few offenders, only their own destruction will stop them. Actually, I expected many more of these offenders to be in this last category, but what I learned about serial rape seems to be different than what many writers have led us to believe. How much can we learn from these experts-by-experience?

Specifically, the primary mission of most serial rapists is to have immediate sexual contact with a female, any female. Some rapists say that their victims had a hand in their own rape and others blame friends or peers. A few rapists explain control and anger as their motivation to rape, while another group describes a god-like supremacy over their victims as their objective. Lastly, some rapists imply that their own fantasy led them to rape.

Predatory rapists explain the role violence played in their attacks as fitting into one of the following categories: nonviolence, intimidation, moderate, limited, and ultimate violence. While the results show several descriptions of murder and necrophilla, violence was selective and used sparingly by serial rapists. The most frequently mentioned method of victim selection was victim vulnerability. The idea of vulnerability demonstrates that violence in and by itself may not be a priority for rapists. When rapists think a female could not or would not resist an attack and an opportunity prevailed by circumstance or manipulation, they will attack regardless of the time of day, whose company she's in, her age, or her circumstance. Offenders continually survey their social environments for prey. Their target techniques are largely in one of the following categories: easy prey, random, and situational. Mostly, how an offender perceives his potential victim affects his decision to attack, and how she responds during the attack will affect its outcome.

Predators attack females for the purpose of physical exploitation including sexual contact; they are in the serious business of fulfilling needs. Predators make few mistakes when they hunt down another person especially another person who seems to be vulnerable. The American criminal justice system must seriously deal with these offenders at a mature and responsible level. What is recommended is effective prevention and persuasive punishment.

Part of the problem is that politically correct thinkers explain criminality through exquisite explanations. Controlling criminals is making a lot of hard choices. One of those choices is realizing that politically correct theory has little to do with criminal reality. The fact is that throughout the history of mankind, there have always been predators. Chances are -- that's the way it will always be; we can't apprehend them all and even if we did, that doesn't mean they won't strike again. We don't have to become their victims, and we don't have help children become monsters. Fighting back is the first line of defense for females.[3]

Equally important, I can't help noticing that many serial rapists embrace evil as an excuse to commit unspeakable acts. Many criminals embrace and internalize the evil in American society which in turn reinforces and often rewards conduct that hints at societal destruction. Does this popular and reinforced image of violent behavior raise another question much like the ugly head of a cross-eyed creature lurking on a different plane of existence that sees its wickedness through a mask of sanity? Has public violence become private violence and is it heading toward collective violence.[4] Like drug traffickers who claim they give customers what they want, rapists, too, suggest that they supply experiences for their prey to become victims. The fact is, many vulnerable females play the role of a victim when attacked. The victim is not to blame. However, females, due in part to the popular media, have learned to be victims or helpless when attacked.

As well, America's youth are traumatized by violence and the antiseptic misery of the underprivileged. It's fashionable to dress and behave like lower class gangsters. Fear entrepreneurs portray violence and sexual exploitation as an appropriate lifestyle. They maintain that serial rapists have the physical and intellectual ability to destroy their victims, and what's more -- they want to. The truth is, they are wrong. Women are not helpless or dumb. Most have both the physical ability and the intelligence to end an attack. The edge an offender has over his victim is not physical strength but surprise. Most serial rapists require surprise since most serial rapists are actually weak men who have no desire for violence. There are a number of rape attempts that were ended by the women who fought back without a gun or a badge, say government statistics.

Law and morals must be preserved should we want to control violent crime. The criminal justice system must become effective and morally spirited should we wish to proceed into the 21st century as a safe society.

Serial rapists are self-indulgent people pursuing objectives without regard for the welfare of others or themselves, at least that is what they want others to believe. Reading between the lines of their self-reports, it sounds as if they want immediate relief from their frustrations, their "itch." They took the quickest way to relieve themselves through forcible rape much like a junkie takes a hit or an alcoholic takes a drink. How can society handle serial rapists especially when something inside them pushes them to feed a dependence? Maybe they should be classified as sexual addicts. It is a matter of record that some sexual offenders have been medically treated with depo-provera (female hormones) and some of those offenders seem to respond favorably. It's called chemical castration. Recently the state of California passed a law which will allow authorities to inject pedophiles with depo-provera to reduce their sexual drives by reducing testosterone levels. They all won't respond positively to the drug, but understanding that serial rapists like most sexual offenders can never be rehabilitated, society must try different methods of control. Scholars today put sexual offenders into psychological or sociological categories explaining that they, too, were victimized as youngsters or adults instead of supporting serious methods of control.

Sexual offenders are exactly where they want to be in their lives, doing exactly what they want to do. They rape to feel comfortable with themselves and the world around them. Serial rape is nourishment, and without it they feel that they would suffocate and die. The more they rape, the greater number of rapes necessary to satisfy their appetite. Once imprisoned, they go through a physical and psychological process that resembles the withdrawal experiences of a drug addict. They may rape in prison, but since their victims are men, their appetite is rarely satisfied. The itch is on the roof of a Mack transfer track, and as it runs over the chest of a rapist, he tries to scratch. A medical model of confinement might be helpful if its operators would remember that their clients are predators and not victims and that the likelihood of them curing serial offenders will never happen. The answer is control.

The criminal justice community must come to the realization that they can not control crime by themselves. They must enter into a real partnership with the community. Therefore, my first recommendation for the criminal justice community is a joint venture between the police and the community. This partnership includes equal responsibility and equal authority under the guidance of professional law enforcement officers. All sexual offenders must be identified to the community and kept away from vulnerable individuals. Above all, police power must be enhanced, plea-bargaining must be eliminated, mandatory life sentences must be initiated with no early release, and capital punishment should be an immediate consequence (after one appeal) of all newly convicted chronic sexual offenders.

---

[1] See Marcus Felson's (1998) review of violence suggesting that all violence is in some sense rational and goal driven. An offender might commit violence to (1) make someone comply with his wishes (to fulfill sexual desires). (2) To restore justice as he sees it (righteous rapists). Or to (3) assert and protect his own identity (sadistic rapist). While these categories may seem an inadequate and incomplete explanation of serial rape motivations, it is clear that there could be a worthwhile discussion here relative to a theoretical explanation. Nonetheless, these categories might merely represent an interpretation or assessment of the conduct of an offender during his rape attacks suggesting that these categories do little to further a causal understanding of the mission itself. It is for that reason that forced sex with a female is more likely to process psychological and physiological addictive properties yet to be accepted by the general public.

[2] See Bart and O'Brien (1985) for a closer look at how victims feel when they don't fight back.

[3] For an in depth look at this idea see Bart & O'Brien (1985).

[4] See Pinilla-Esteban (1993) for a discussion on private violence becoming collective or public violence. Also see Weiner, Zahn, and Sagi, (1990) for a closer look at this perspective.

APPENDIX I

ABOUT THE PRISON

The inmate population was interviewed in a maximum security prison within walking distance from the state capital building of South Carolina. When someone first saw this penitentiary, they might stare at its wired walls which were easily dwarfed by several antediluvian buildings surrounded by two modern tinted-glass rifle towers. New inmate arrivals learned quickly that this prison transcended their worst nightmares about prison life. It was filled with wetness, whaled cries, and endless halls going nowhere. To enter some cells and rooms even short men had to duck. The prison was built in 1871 and, over the years, it hasn't changed other than a few additions built by inmate labor. Its average daily population was 1,340 at the time of this study, which was about 300 inmates over its designed capacity. Inmates slept on cots everywhere including a once poorly supplied library. All parts of the prison were connected by one outside tunnel which was locked down when necessary, but guards and inmates stood idly in open unprotected areas. Part of the unofficial policy of the correctional system was that inmates were "property of the State of South Carolina and that means we can do anything we want to them," said one captain. Security and daily routines changed continually depending on the orientation of the officer in charge. Some units were safer than others and well managed by caring correctional officers and staff. But drugs, sex and misery were pervasive.

Overall. the day began at 6:00 a.m. and ended at 10:00 p.m. There were five inmate counts a day. Three meals were served in a centrally located dining area; there was a small educational area and a church (which also doubled as a sleeping area for some new arrivals). All inmates were given a security level in addition to their maximum custody risk rating. Inmates ate in shifts, so there was constant movement in and out of the dining room. They prayed in similar groups, too. Inmates moved around within their security level living unit (except segregation), but they could not enter the tunnel since each unit was locked down. Many of the units were further segregated. For example, while 200 inmates were in 'A' unit consisting of five floors of cells, with 35 inmates on each floor, each floor could be seen from the ground floor since the open hall in front of the cells was enclosed with chicken-coop wire. Convicted rapists were segregated to their own units and few inmates had access to their floors. Aggressive classified inmates were segregated from passive classified inmates, but easy-going classified inmates were celled with either group. The highest security level was on the 5th floor and those inmates could not leave that floor or their cells during certain hours. Correctional officers were stationed inside each unit to control inmate movement. Relations between inmates and between inmates and staff was often tense, especially during the blistering summer months since air conditioning and other methods of venting were nonexistent or inoperable. Many men, both staff and inmates alike, were seen gagging and sometimes vomiting in the pass ways.

A few hundred inmates were in protective custody; they had freedom of movement but only within their living unit. The general prison population, however, did not have access to this unit. Other inmates were in 'segregation' which meant they were locked down 23 hours per day allowing one hour of exercise. They ate and slept alone, and never saw anyone other than an assigned officer. These individuals, such as Pee Wee Gaskins who was finally executed when he had taken a contract to kill another inmate and fulfilled his contract, were the highest security level in this prison and required special attention and isolation. None of those inmates were part of this study.

Most of the time inmates lifted weights, played sports in the large field facing the city's business district several blocks away built on a ridge, or went to technical or academic school. Few worked. Most were idle. Visitation was once a week, and security routines often changed. It was rumored that inmates had sex with strangers and got anything else they wanted in the visitation areas. During the time of this study, a female graduate student was caught throwing a bag of cocaine over the wall by the expressway. Inside this walled community, everybody knew everything about everybody else, including staff and administrators. Information was part of their way of life and inmates used that information to try extorting staff members when it served their purpose.

Unlike typical prisons, this maximum facility had few if any gangs. However, if someone attacked an inmate from Charleston, South Carolina then other inmates from Charleston would defend him. Likewise, those from Columbia defended each other and so on. Largely, race in this prison was not an issue unless you were a correctional officer. There were many stabbings between inmates, some serious, but not many serious incidents between inmates and officers. Inmate personal relationships were numerous, and many inmates belonged to many different informal groups. Inmates did not have furloughs away from the prison or conjugal visits.

The tension and regulations of Attica and Stateville were not present, probably because the South Carolina rank and file officers were inmate-friendly and relationships existed between custodians and inmates. Most officers and inmates came from similar environments and many were black as was the inmate population. The administrators and brass (lieutenants and above in rank), however, always had a problem with both the rank and file correctional officers and staff and the inmates. The rudeness of inmates and the rank and file correctional officers of the northern states, especially Attica, was less pronounced in the South Carolina prison. In a sense, I felt safer walking through the tunnel to the educational department even though it was often filled with hundreds of inmates, then when I encountered ten well-guarded inmates lined up for medicine at Attica or Stateville. During minor or routine riots, I was safer among my inmate students and group-encounter members at all the prisons I worked at, than with management or brass, such as the captain mentioned above. This prison was finally closed in 1993 and its inmates were sent to other prisons within the system.

APPENDIX 2

STUDENT-INTERVIEWERS

Each student-interviewer recruited five volunteers from his cellblock to discuss predatory crimes prior to incarceration. These discussions were designed to keep the subjects and interviewers comfortable as they revealed predatory accounts. Typical interviews lasted over an hour and were conducted in various locations throughout the prison. Neither the researchers nor the subjects received any monetary gain for their participation; however, the student-interviewers received three university credit hours for completion of the course.

I also conducted twenty interviews with inmates and had the help of correctional officers in locating volunteers who knew something about predatory crime. To insure confidentiality, those interviews were conducted in a prison classroom. Although, I never knew any of the names of the inmates I interviewed, my reputation as a prison teacher and group facilitator holding many inmate confidences apparently helped the interview process as many of the participants seemed uninhibited after several minutes of general discussion. During the interview, I entered their statements into a computer. if they consented. All but four did. My data and the data of the student-interviewers were similar.

A total of 85 inmates were interviewed in the spring of 1992. Of the 85 total interviews, only 61 were considered reliable. The unreliability was due to the following factors: One student-interviewer allegedly interviewed 5 inmates but his interviews were challenged by his peers; 3 inmates were interviewed twice; 2 informants admitted to only male rape; 1 inmate raped only children, 8 informants had not admitted to predatory rape, and 5 cases were so confusing or poorly written by student-interviewers that I did not include them. The subject

108

participants were individual male prisoners incarcerated in a high custody facility who reported serial rape accounts before their confinement. I have 316 accounts of serial rape as reported by the participants of this study, but expect that the actual number of serial rapes is closer to 1,708. I determined that number by reviewing the data. Since the average age of the participants was 32 at the time of the interviews and most of the descriptions of the participants characterized criminal lifestyle experiences at 18 years of age, two rapes a year over a 14 year period (28 times 61 = 1,708) might be closer to the truth.

Criminal Validity

I collected data through inmate-interviewers, conducted twenty interviews myself for purposes of validity, and discussed all the findings with other offenders and other prison professionals in other high custody prisons. Most indicated that the accounts of the participants as accumulated by the inmate-interviewers and myself appeared realistic, and they were able to relate the findings to their experiences with other apprehended predators they had known.

APPENDIX 3

TYPE OF QUESTIONS

I used A. Nicholas Groth's "Protocol for the Clinical Assessment of the Offender's Sexual Behaviors" as a guide for the questions. Topics included were:

1. Premeditation

To what extend did you plan the offense? Did you set out in search of a victim with a deliberate intent to commit sexual assault? Did the idea suddenly come to mind when an opportunity presented itself? In terms of importance before a rapist attacks a female he doesn't know, what should he do first: Rank order the following if 1 is the first thing and 6 the last or just say you don't know: be sure she's alone, old enough, going to like it, drunk/stoned, not a fighter, pretty.

2. Victim Selection

What were the descriptive characteristics (age, race, sex, situation, physical characteristics) of the victim, and what part did each play in the your selection? Was there a relationship with the victim prior to the incident? What was it about the physical characteristics of the victim that made her the victim? Could you have had sex with anyone else at the time? Can you describe the victim? Do you recall what she looked like?

3. Style of Attack

How did you gain control over your victim? Did you use description and entrapment, threat or intimidation, physical force or violence, or some combination of those techniques? How did you gain sexual access to your victim? Did you render your victim helpless through drugs or alcohol? Did you make promises to the victim that you couldn't keep?

4. Accompanying Fantasies

What were you fantasizing during the attack? Was the victim in your fantasy identifiable? Did the attack go as you dreamt it? When did these fantasies first begin? How often did they repeat themselves?

5. Role of Aggression

How seriously did you want to hurt your victim? Under what conditions would you resort to physical force during the rape? How excising was the real force that you used? Did it turn you on?

6. Sexual Behavior

What was going on sexually during the rape (kissing, fondling, masturbating, breast sucking, digital penetration, vaginal intercourse, oral intercourse, or anal contract, etc.) Did you tie the victim? Did you ask the victim to act out any role or get into various sexual positions? Did you get off? Did she phase you? Were you frustrated or disappointed after the rape? How long did it last? How did you think she felt during and after the offense?

7. Contributing Factors

What triggered the rape? Responsibility: are you admitting to the rape?

8. Recidivism

In your dreams about how many times might you of raped a girl you didn't know?

9. Deterrence

What could the victim do to stop rape from happening.

10. Martial Relations

When you were a free man, how was your sex life at home?

APPENDIX 4

WHO WERE THE OFFENDERS IN THIS STUDY?

According to the responses of the offenders, the average respondent was 32 years old (see Table 5). Fifty-six percent (34) of the participants were black, 41% (25) were white, and 3% (2) were Hispanic whose average education was 8th grade, prior to this conviction. Thirty-one percent (19) were married, 69% (42) were single and/or divorced, and 66% (40) reported having a regular sex life prior to incarceration. Sixty-two percent (38) of the respondents reported that they held a menial job (such as house care maintenance and auto service station workers), 10% (6) reported a white collar job (such as a CPA and a high school teacher), and 27% (17) reported being unemployed prior to incarceration. Yet, 43% (26) of both the employed and the unemployed reported earning most of their spending money from an illegal source such as hustling, theft, and drug trafficking. The typical respondent reported being arrested 3.4 times and he had served an average of 84 months.

Sixty-six percent (40) of the participants had been convicted of a crime of violence (homicide, armed robbery, aggravated assault, and sexual assault). What the participants reported and what the records of the participants showed about their convictions were similar. Specifically, 5% (3) were convicted of homicide (murder and manslaughter), 5% (3) armed robbery, 28% (17) of aggravated assault, and 28% (17) of sexual assault (Of interest, only two of the 17 individuals convicted of sexual violations used physical force before, during, or after their sexual assault. Also, despite several self-reports of serial rape with a child, none of these offenders were convicted of a sexual violation on a child). Also, 35%

(21) were convicted of a crime of nonviolence. More specifically, 18% (11) were convicted of a parole violation 18% (11), 10% (6) larceny, and 7% (4) drug/alcohol related crimes.

Table 5   Average Characteristics of Offenders   (N=61)

CHARACTERISTICS	AVERAGE/PERCENT	Range/numbers
Age	32	18-52
Race		
Black	56%	34
White	41%	25
Hispanic	3%	2
Education	8	2-17
Married	31%	19
Single/Divorced	69%	42
Regular Sex Life	66%	40
Menial Jobs	62%	38
White Collar Jobs	10%	6
Unemployed	27%	17
Illegal Incomes	43%	26
Arrests	3.4	1-14
Months Served	84	1-135
Convictions		
Homicide	5%	3
Armed Robbery	5%	3
Aggravated Assault	28%	17
Sexual Assault	28%	17
Parole Violation	18%	11
Larceny	10%	6
Drug/Alcohol	7%	4

* due to rounding, percents do not equal 100%

114

Data Collection

Data collection and analysis proceeded simultaneously in keeping with Barney Glasser and Anselm Strauss' perspectives of "grounded theory." Both process and products of research were shaped from the statements made by the offenders. Fresh theoretical interpretation was sought from offender statements and checking inmate records and a questionnaire helped gather information about race, age, arrest rates, and so on. Careful review of the account-sets (316 accounts from 61 participants), I chose one typical description that best characterized each set (participant). Once completed, the typical descriptions were compared, analyzed, and similar descriptions were put into three typologies (motive, target selections, and violence). Using a number of tests including ideas shared by colleagues and by correctional personnel, those descriptions produced seven mutually exclusive categories presenting a motive typology: lust, righteous, peer, control/anger, supremacy, fantasy and unclear (see Chapter 4 and 5). Similar tests were used to develop a target selection typology comprised of four mutually exclusive categories: easy prey, random, situational and not sure (see Chapter 6). Finally, a violence used typology was developed comprised of six mutually exclusive categories: unclear, nonviolence, intimidation, moderate, limited, and ultimate (see Chapter 7). When these typologies were compared with academic and mainstream literature, distinctive differences emerged.

Interviews

The average interview lasted approximately fifty minutes with a range from fifteen minutes to two hours. An inmate's age, education, and other demographic questions were answered on a questionnaire given each inmate prior to his interview. The inmate-interviewers wrote the statements that applied to serial rape and other crime as they spoke with the offenders they interviewed. When I interviewed 20 offenders, I first tried to tape-record their conversations, but the offenders were reluctant to speak about their affairs. Yet, they allowed me to enter their statements into a computer, providing there were other statements on the screen.

APPENDIX 5

RACE OF VICTIMS

All of the offenders said that they had raped white females more often than females from other races. Also, 75% (26) of the black rapists and 3% (2) of the Hispanic respondents described only white victims in all of their predatory rape accounts.

The fact that majority of black and Hispanic offenders were allegedly interracial rapists conflicts with virtually most scientific study results.[1] One reason for this inconsistency relating to interracial rapes could be that offenders tend to be incarcerated more often depending upon the race of their victims as opposed to the seriousness of their criminal acts. Thus, black on black crime may be different from black on black conviction rates. What is also known about rape in general, depending upon whose estimates you want to believe, is that fewer black women report rape than white women. Female rape victims in victimization reports confirm interracial activity, but, if some women have different perceptions about how others view the race of their attacker, some women might lie about it. Other reasons could be that the subjects were lying about their victims in order to enhance their reputations with inmate-interviewees because white women victims may be perceived as more valuable prey, than black victims. Also, all of the white offenders said that they had raped only white victims. White women are targeted more often than black women because black women tend to be less vulnerable than white women. As a group, black women might not accept the idea of a learned helplessness as often as white women, thus black women as a group were less desirable as a target.

Lastly, the participants revealed few family ties as adults and perceived themselves as loners during childhood. Only 7% of the subjects reported that they were first-time violent offenders. Most of the participants represent the habitual abuser and prisoner.

[1] For more insight on this disparity read Bernard Headley (1983).

REFERENCES

Abramson, I.Y., Seligman, M.E.P., & Teasdale, J.D. (1978). "Learned Helplessness in Humans: Critique and Reformulation". *Journal of Abnormal Psychology*, 87, 49-74.

Amir, M. (1971). *Patterns in Forcible Rape.* Chicago: University of Chicago Press.

Athens, L.H. (1980). *Violent Criminal Acts and Actors.* Boston: Routledge & Kegan Paul.

Averill, J.R. (1993). "Illusions of Anger". In R.B. Felson and J.T. Tedeschi (Eds.). *Aggression and Violence: Social Interactionist Perspectives.* (Pp. 171-192). Washington DC: APA.

Bandura, A.(1973). *Aggression: A Social Learning Process.* Englewood Cliffs, NJ: Prentice Hall.

Bart, P. & O'Brien, P. (1985). *Stopping Rape: Successful Survival Strategies.* Elmsford, NY: Pergamon Press.

Berger, P.L. (1963). *Invitation to Sciology: A Hmanistic Prspective.* NY: Doubleday.

Belknap, J. (1996). *The Invisible Woman: Gender, Crime, and Justice.* NY: Wadsworth.

Blumer. H. (1969). *Symbolic Interactionism.* Englewood Cliffs, NJ: Prentice Hall.

Brownmiller, S. (1975). *Against Our Will: Men, Women, and Wape.* NY: Simon & Schuster.

Bureau of Justice Statistics. (1997). *Sourcebook of Criminal Justice Statistics -1994.* Washington DC: US Department of Justice, Office of Justice Programs. Available: [On-line] http://www.albany.edu/sourcebook/

Burgess, L., L., & Burgess, A.,W. (1974). *The Victim of Rape: Institutional Reactions.* NY: John Wiley & Sons.

Cohen, M., Garofalo, R, Boucher, R., & Seghorn, T. (1971). "The Psychology of Rapists". *Seminars in Psychiatry, 3,* 307-327.

Denno, D. (1990). *Biology and Violence: From Birth to Adulthood.* NY: Cambridge University Press.

Douglas, J., & Olshaker, M. (1995). *Mind Hunter.* NY: Pocket Star Books.

Eichental, D., & Jacobs, J. (1991). "Enforcing the Criminal Law in State Prisons". *Justice Quartery,* 8, 283-303.

Ellis, L. 1989. *Theories of Rape.* New York: Hemisphere.

Elkin, F., & Handel, G. (1984). *The Child and Society: The Process of Socialization.* NY: Random House.

Eysenck, H.,& Gudjonsson, G. (1989). *The Causes and Cures of Criminality.* NY: Plenum.

Felson, M. (1998). *Crime and Everyday Life.* Thousand Oaks, CA: Pine Forge Press.

Felson, R.B., & Krohn, M. (1990). "Motives for Rape". *Journal of Research in Crime and Delinquency, 27* (3), 222-241.

Felson, R.B. (1993). "Motives for Sexual Coercion." In Richard B. Belson and James T. Tedeschi (Eds.). *Aggression and Violence: Social Interactionist Perspectives.* Washington, D.C.: APA.

Frost, B. (1995). "Prosecution and Sentencing". In James Q. Wilson and Joan Petersilia (Eds.). *Crime.* San Francisco, CA: ICS Press. pp. 363-387.

Gaskins, D. "Pee Wee" with Wilton, E. (1994). *Final Truth.* NY: Windsor.

Giacoia, O. (1992). "Fatality of Violence and Fecundity of Thinking". *Perspectives,* 15, 107-117.

Glaser, B., & Strauss, A. (1967). *The Discovery of The Grounded Theory: Strategies for Qualitative Research.* Chicago: Aldine.

Goldstein, A.P. (1990). *Delinquents on Delinquency.* Champaign, IL:

Research Press.

Gollmar, R. (1981). *America's Most Bizarre Murderer: Edward Gein*. NY: Pinnacle.

Gottfredson, M., & Hirschi, T. (1990). *A general theory of crime*. Stanford, CA: Stanford.

Gordon, M.T., & Riger, S. (1989). *The Female Fear: The Social Cost of Rape*. NY: Free Press.

Groth, N.A. (1979). *Men Who Rape: The Psychology of The Offender*. NY: Plenum Press.

Groth, N.A., & Burgess, A.W. (1980). "Male Rape: Offenders and Victims". *American Journal of Psychiatry*, 137(7), 806-810.

Hazelwood, R., & Warren, J. (1990). "Rape: The Criminal Behavior of The Serial Rapist". *FBI Law Enforcement Bulletin*. February, pp. 11-15.

Hazelwood R., Reboussin,R.. & Warren, J. (1989). "Serial Rape: Correlates of Increased Aggression and The Relationship of Offender Pleasure to Victim Resistance". *Journal of Interpersonal Violence* 4(1), 65-78.

Headley, R. (1983). "Black on Black Crime: The myth and The Reality". *Crime and Social Justice, 20*, 50-61.

Heller, A., Stamatiou, W., & Puntscher-Riekmann, S. (1993). "The Limits to Natural Law and The Paradox of Evil". *Journal fur Sozialforschung, 33*(2), 107-120.

Holmes, R. (1991). *Sex Crimes*. CA: Sage.

Kanin, E. J. (1984). "Date Rape: Unofficial Criminals and Victims". *Victimology 9*, 95-108.

Katz, J. (1988). *Seductions of Crime*. NY: Basic Books.

Katz, F.E.(1993). *Ordinary People and Extraordinary Evil*. NY: State University of NY.

Kruttschnitt, C., Ward, D., & Sheble, M. A. (1987). "Abuse-resistant Youth: Some Factors That May Inhibit Violent Criminal Behavior". *Social Forces,66*(2), 501-519.

Lyman, S. (1978*). Seven Deadly Sins: Society and Evil.* NY: St.Martin's.

Lyman, S., & Scott, (1989). *A Sociology of the Absurd.* Dix Hills, NY: General Hall.

MacKinnon, C. (1987). *Feminism Unmodified.* NY: Wiley.

Medea, A. ,& Thompson, K. (1974). *Against Rape: A Survival Manual for Women: How to Cope With Rape Physically and Emotionally.* NY: Farrar, Straus, and Giraux.

Mills, C. W. (1940, 1963). "Situated Actions and Vocabularies of Motive". In I.L. Horowitz (Ed). *Power, Politics and People: The Collected Essays of C. Wright Mills.* NY: Oxford University Press. pp. 439-452.

Mills, C. W. (1951). *White Collar.* NY: Oxford University Press.

Palmer, C.T. (1988). "Twelve Reasons Why Rape is Not Sexually Motivated: A skeptical Examination". *Journal of Sex Research, 25* (5), 12-30.

Petersilia, J. (1977). *Criminal Careers of Habitual Felons: A Summary Report.* Santa Monica, CA: Rand.

Pinilla-Esteban, D.L.H. (1993). "Public Violence and Private Violence". *Revista Internacional de Sociologia, 5,* 163-173.

Quinsey, V.S., Chaplin, T.S., & Upfold, D. (1984). "Sexual Arousal to Nonsexual Violence and Sadomasochistic Themes Among Rapists and Nonsexual Offenders". *Journal of Consulting Clinical Psychology, 52,* 651-657.

Reid, S.T. (1996). *Crime and Criminology.* Madison, WI: Brown & Benchmark.

Reiman, J. (1995). *The Rich Get Richer and The Poor Get Prison.* NY: Macmillan.

Rule, A. (1980). *The Stranger Beside Me.* NY: New American Library.

Sanday, P. (1981). "The Socio-cultural Context of Rape: A Cross Cultural Study". *Journal of Social Issues, 37,* 5-27.

Samenow, S. (1984). *Inside the Criminal Mind.* NY: Random.

Schmalleger, F. (1998). *Criminology Today.* Englewood Cliffs, NJ: Prentice Hall.

Schwartz, I. (1989). *(In)Justice for Juveniles: Rethinking The Best Interests of The Child.* Lexington, MS: Heath.

Schwendinger, J., & Schwendinger, H. (1983). *Rape and Inequality.* Beverly Hills: Sage Publications.

Scully, D., & Marolla, J. (1984). "Convicted Rapists' Vocabulary of Motive: Excuses and Justifications". *Social Problems, 31,* 530-544.

Scully, D. (1990). *Understanding Sexual Violence.* NY: Putnum.

Seligman, M.E.P. (1975). *Helplessness: On Depression, Development, and Death.* San Francisco, CA: Freeman.

Stevens, D.J. (1998). "Interviews with Women Convicted of Murder: Battered Women Syndrome Revisited". *Victimology.* In Press

Stevens, D.J. (1998b). "Incarcerated Women, Crime and Drug Addiction". *The Criminologist,* 22(1), 3-14.

Stevens, D.J. (1998c). "The Impact of Time-served and Regime on Prisoners' Anticipation of Crime: Female Prisonisation Effects". *The Howard Journal of Criminal Justice,* 37(2), 188-205.

Stevens, D.J. (1998d). "What Do Police Officers Think about Their Jobs". *The Journal: The Voice of Law Enforcement,* 5(1), 60-62.

Stevens, D.J. (1998e). "Mandatory Arrest and Domestic Violence: Attitudes of Victims and Officers". *The Journal: The Voice of Law Enforcement.* In Press.

Stevens, D.J. (1998f). "Explanations of Excessive Force Used During Serial Rape Attacks." *Criminologist,* 22(2), 67-83.

Stevens, D.J. (1998g). "Prisoner Restrictions, Inmate Custodial Relations, and Inmate Attitudes Towards Compliance". *Research and Statistics Branch of the Correctional Service of Canada.* In Press.

Stevens, D.J. (1998h). "Arrest-conviction Barriers of Narcotic Law Enforcement Officers". *The Voice of Law Enforcement.* In press.

124

Stevens, D.J. (1998I). "Correctional Officer Attitudes: Job Satisfaction Levels to Length of Employment." *Corrections Compendium: The National Journal of Correcting*, 23(7), 2-3, 19-20.

Stevens, D.J. (1997a). "Violence and Serial Rape". *Journal of Police and Criminal Psychology*. 12(12), 39-47

Stevens, D.J. (1997b). "Prison Regime and Drugs". *The Howard Journal of Criminal Justice*, 36(1), 14-27.

Stevens, D.J. (1997c). "Influences of Early Childhood Experiences on Subsequent Criminally Violent Behavior". *Studies on Crime and Crime Prevention*, 6(1), 34-50.

Stevens, D.J. (1997d). Communities and Homicide: Why Blacks Resort to Murder". *The Criminologist*, 21(3), 145-157.

Stevens, D.J. (1995a). "Motives of Serial Rapists". *Free Inquiry of Creative Sociology*, 23(2), 117-127.

Stevens, D.J. (1995b). "The Impact of Time Served and Custody Level on Offender Attitudes". *Forum on Corrections Research*, 9, 12-14.

Stevens, D.J. (1994a). "Predatory Rape and Victim Targeting Techniques". *The Social Science Journal*, 31(4), 421-433.

Stevens, D.J. (1994b). "The Depth of Imprisonment and Prisonisation: Levels of Security and Prisoners' Anticipation of Future Violence". *The Howard Journal of Criminal Justice*, 33(2), 137-157.

Stevens, D.J. (1992a). "Research Note: The Death Sentence and Inmate Attitudes". *Crime & Delinquency*, 38, 272-279.

Stevens, D. J. (1992b). "Examining Inmate Attitudes: Do Prisons Deter Crime?" *The State of Corrections - American Correctional Association: 1991*. 272-279.

Stevens, D.J. (1988). "Education: The Assembly". *Urban Education*, 23 (1), 107-114.

Storaska, F. (1975). *How To Say No To A Rapist And Survive*. NY:Random House.

Sussman L., & Bordwell, S. (1981). *The Rapist File*. NY: Chelsea House.

Tock, H., & Adams, K. (1989). *The Disturbed Violent Offender*. New Haven, MA: Yale University Press.

Thomas, W.I., & Thomas, D. (1928). *The Child in America: Behavior Problems and Programs*. NY: Knopf.

Weiner, N.A., Zahn, M.A., & Sagi, R.J. (1990). *Violence: Patterns, Causes, Public Policy*. FL: Harcourt Race Jovanovich Publishers.

Zukier, H. (1994). "The Twisted Road to Genocide: On The Psychological Development of Evil During The Holocaust". *Social Research*, 61(2), 423-455.

INDEX

Printed in the United States
77213LV00004B/239

9 780595 146635